Risk and Return in Transportation and Other US and Global Industries

by

Manolis G. Kavussanos

City University Business School, London, United Kingdom

and

Stelios N. Marcoulis

Laiki Investments, Cyprus Popular Bank Group, Nicosia, Cyprus and City University Business School, London, United Kingdom

SPRINGER-SCIENCE+BUSINESS MEDIA, B.V.

A C.I.P. Catalogue record for this book is available from the Library of Congress.

DOI 10.1007/978-1-4757-6441-3

Printed on acid-free paper

RISK AND RETURN IN TRANSPORTATION
AND OTHER US AND GLOBAL INDUSTRIES

We would like to dedicate this book to our parents:

George Kavussanos and Erofili Kavussanou

and

Nikos Marcoulis and Eleni Marcouli

The authors are grateful to

City University Business School

and to

Cyprus Popular Bank

for providing financial support for this project

It would be impossible to name everyone who has helped us over the years to put the research which is underlying this book together. However, we would like to thank participants' comments in presentations made of parts of the book at the IAME conferences in Vancouver, Canada and in London, UK, and also at the Shipping Economists' Group, UK Chamber of Shipping. Thanks are also due to Sarah Baylis and Amir Alizadeh for helping us put the final pieces of the work together in a single book. Professors Mario Levis, Mezianne Lasfer, Kevin Cullinane and Hercules Haralambides have provided helpful comments, while Angelos Arkoulis has helped with the data and has co-authored chapter 8 of this book. Of course any remaining errors or omissions are our own responsibility.

About the Authors

Dr. Manolis Kavussanos holds a BSc and MSc in Economics from Queen Mary & Westfield and Birkbeck Colleges of the University of London, and a Ph.D. (1993) in Applied Economics from City University. He joined City University in November 1987 and has held positions as ESRC Management Teaching Fellow, Lecturer and Senior Lecturer in Applied Economics and Reader in Shipping Economics and Finance. He has lectured in the past in subject areas such as Maritime Business, Shipping Investment & Finance, Economic Modelling, Quantitative Methods and in the PhD programme in Financial Economics. In 1996 he helped launch the MSc in Trade, Transport and Finance at the Department of Shipping Trade and Finance and has since become the Director of this program.

He has written extensively in the areas of shipping and finance and has been the author of numerous papers published or forthcoming in top international refereed journals, including monographs and journal guest volumes. His research work on shipping and financial markets has been presented in international conferences held in the UK, Italy, Greece, China, US, Canada and Australia, amongst others, and in professional meetings such as the UK and Turkish Chambers of Shipping, amongst others.

In the above work, he has consistently introduced modern econometric methods in examining relevant shipping economics and finance issues. This has resulted in published pioneering work in such areas as risk measurement and management techniques in shipping, including freight derivatives, equity pricing of shipping stocks, seasonality and general microstructure issues of shipping freight markets and vessel markets as well as forecasting. A number of Ph.D. and numerous MSc theses have also been produced under his supervision.

Dr. Kavussanos is a well known member of the shipping and finance community, and as such has been involved as guest editor and serves on the editorial board of academic journals in his field; he has acted as research proposal evaluator for organisations like the Commission of the European Communities and the Central Research Funding agency of Hong-Kong. He has refereed for a number of well-known academic journals and has been external examiner for Ph.D. theses in other institutions apart from CUBS, such as the University of London and Erasmus University, Rotterdam. He has also been on Scientific Committees and has provided consultancy services for private companies involved in shipping and finance, and has also been included in the Marquis publication 'Who is Who in the World'.

Dr. Stelios Marcoulis holds a BSc in Business Studies and an MSc in Shipping Trade and Finance from City University Business School, an MSc in Accounting and Finance from the London School of Economics and a Ph.D. (1999) in Finance, also from City University Business School.

He joined Laiki Investments, the investment banking arm of the Cyprus Popular Bank Group in 1996 and is currently a Senior Corporate Finance Manager at the Company's Investment Banking Division. He has been dealing with corporate finance work such as initial public offerings (IPOs), corporate bond issues, financial restructuring and company valuations in industries such as pharmaceuticals, shipping, manufacturing and trading, among others.

Before joining Laiki Investments he held a research position for two and a half years, as Research Assistant to Professor Costas Th. Grammenos, at the then International Centre for Shipping, Trade and Finance of City University Business School. During his time there, his research interests covered areas regarding the financing of shipping companies through the capital markets of the world. A number of MSc theses have also been produced under his supervision. He is currently a visiting fellow at the Department of Shipping, Trade and Finance of City University Business School, his main area of interest being the valuation of shipping companies for corporate finance purposes.

He has several publications, as co-author, in the areas of shipping and finance, which have been published in international refereed journals and journal guest volumes. His research work on shipping and financial markets has also been presented in international conferences held in the UK, Greece, and Canada.

CONTENTS

LIST OF FIGURES

LIST OF TABLES

LIST OF ABBREVIATIONS

ADF:	Augmented Dickey Fuller
AIC:	Akaike Information Criterion
APT:	Arbitrage Pricing Theory
AR:	Autoregressive
ARMA:	Autoregressive Moving Average
ARIMA:	Autoregressive Integrated Moving Average
BLUE:	Best Linear Unbiased Estimators
CAPM:	Capital Asset Pricing Model
DOD:	Department of Defence
DOT:	Department of Transportation
GLS:	Generalised Least Squares
HSBC:	Hong Kong and Shanghai Banking Corporation
IAME:	International Association of Maritime Economists
I(d):	Integrated variable of order d
LMSR:	Large, Medium Speed RO/RO's
LP:	Liquefied Petroleum
MA:	Moving Average
ML:	Maximum Likelihood
MLE:	Maximum Likelihood Estimator
MLSQ:	Multiple Least Squares Regression Models
MSCI	Morgan Stanley Capital International
NYSE:	The New York Stock Exchange
ODS:	Operating Differential Subsidy
OLS:	Ordinary Least Squares Model
RO/RO:	Roll-on/Roll-off
RRF:	Ready Reserve Force
RSS:	Residual Sum of Squares
RRSS:	Restricted Residual Sum of Squares
URSS:	Unrestricted Residual Sum of Squares
S&P 500:	Standard and Poor's 500 Index
SBIC:	Schwarz Bayesian Information Criterion
SEC:	Securities Exchange Commission
SIC:	Standard Industrial Classification
SURE:	Seemingly Unrelated Regression Equations
UPS:	United Parcel Service
VAR:	Vector Autoregressive
WACC:	Weighted Average Cost of Capital

LIST OF SYMBOLS

+ve:	Positive
-ve:	Negative
$\otimes$:	Kronecker product in matrix operations
$<$:	Smaller than
$>$:	Greater than
$\forall$:	for all
α_j:	Alpha of company j
A/BE:	Asset Value to Book Value of Equity
A/ME:	Asset Value to Market Value of Equity
β_j:	Beta of company j
$\hat{\beta}_j$:	Estimate of Beta of company j
$\tilde{b}$:	Maximum Likelihood estimator of b
BE/ME:	Book Value to Market Value of Equity
$\chi^2(n)$:	chi-squared distribution with n degrees of freedom
C:	Monthly US Consumption
CG:	Consumption Growth
CPI:	US Consumer Price Index
C (X,Y):	Covariance between variables X and Y
CV:	Coefficient of Variation
ΔX_t:	Change in value of variable X from period t-1 to t
d_{jt}:	Monthly dividend of company j
d_t:	Binary (Dummy) Variable taking values of 1 and 0
dG10FX	G-10 aggregate exchange rate against the US dollar
dG7IP	weighted average monthly industrial production in the G-7 countries
dOIL	changes in the US dollar price per barrel of Brent Oil
dTED	3-month Eurodollar minus 3-month US Treasury Bill rate
DW:	Durbin Watson Statistic
Dw:	Weight of Debt in the Capital Structure
ε_{ijt}:	Error term of population regression line
e_{ijt}:	Residual term of sample regression line
Ew:	Weight of Equity in the Capital Structure
E:	(nT x 1) vector of error terms ε
E/P:	Earnings to Price ratio
F(n,m):	F distribution with n and m degrees of freedom
I:	Inflation
I_{it}	index value of industry i at time t
I_T:	(T x T) Identity matrix
INTRCPT:	Intercept of the regression equation
Kd:	Cost of Debt
Ke:	Cost of Equity
KU:	Kurtosis

LGB:	End of Period Return on Long - Term Government Bonds
ln(z):	Natural Logarithm of z
μ:	Population mean of a set of data
ME:	Market Value of Equity
MIP:	Monthly Industrial Production
O:	Monthly Oil Brent price index
OG:	Oil Prices Growth
π:	= 3.14
Π:	Population proportion
p:	Sample proportion
P_{ijt}:	Share Price of Company j in industry i at period (month) t
P_{ijt-1}:	Share Price of Company j in industry at period (month) t-1
PW_t	world equity index value in $US
Q(p) :	Box-Pierce Q Statistic for pth order autocorrelation
R_{ft}:	The Risk Free Rate
R_{ijt}:	Holding Period Return on the Equity of Company j in i at industry Period t
$\overline{R}_j$:	Arithmetic mean return (over time) of equity of company j in industry i
$\rho(R_j,R_M)$:	Correlation coefficient between variable R_j and variable R_M
ρ_k:	Population Autocorrelation Coefficient of Order k
r:	Sample Correlation Coefficient
r_k:	Sample Autocorrelation Coefficient of Order k
R_{Mt}:	Holding Period Return on the Market in Period t
R^2:	R squared or coefficient of multiple determination
$\overline{R}^2$:	R-bar squared or adjusted coefficient of multiple determination
R^2_u:	R^2 of the unrestricted model
R^2_R:	R^2 of the restricted model
$\lvert R_{Mt}\rvert$:	Absolute value of R_{Mt}
σ^2:	Population variance of a set of data
$\tilde{\sigma}^2$:	Maximum Likelihood Estimator of σ^2
$\hat{\sigma}^2$:	Ordinary Least Squares Estimator of σ^2
$\hat{\sigma}$:	Estimated standard error of regression
σ_{Mt}:	Standard Deviation of Market Return
$\sum_{t=1}^{T} X_t$:	Summation of values of variable X over its range, t=1,…,T
$\Sigma = [\sigma_{ij}]$:	Variance-Covariance Matrix
$\hat{\Sigma} = [\hat{\sigma}_{ij}]$:	Estimated Σ, the variance covariance matrix
S:	Sum of Squared Residuals
SE:	Standard Error of a variable
$\hat{SE}$ (b):	Estimated Standard Error of coefficient b
SD:	Standard Deviation
SK:	Skewness
t(n):	Student's t – distribution with n degrees of freedom
t-stat:	t statistic

t:	Marginal Tax Rate
TB_t:	The One Month Treasury Bill Rate
TLP	weighted average G-7 inflation rate
TS:	The Term Structure of Interest Rates
UdTED	unexpected component of dTED
UdOIL	unexpected component of dOIL
UdG10FX	unexpected component of dG10FX
UdG7IP	unexpected component of dG7IP
UCG:	Unanticipated Changes in Consumption Growth
UI:	Unanticipated Changes in Inflation
UTLP	unexpected component of TLP
UOG:	Unanticipated Changes in Oil Prices Growth
UTS:	Unanticipated Changes in the Term Structure
$WDRET_t$	$=\ln(PW_t/PW_{t-1})-USTB_t$
WDRET	return on the MSCI World Equity Index
$XR_{jt}=R_{jt}-R_{ft}$:	Excess Holding Period Return on the Equity of Company j in Period t
$XR_{Mt}=R_{Mt}-R_{ft}$:	Excess Holding Period Return on the Market in Period t
X:	(T x k) matrix
X':	Transpose of matrix X
$\underline{x}$:	(T x 1) vector of time series observations on variable x
Ω:	Real positive definite symmetric matrix.

CHAPTER 1: BOOK OVERVIEW

1.1 Aim of the Book

The aim of this book is to investigate the risk - return behaviour of stock returns of the water transportation industry in the US[1] along several dimensions, such as time; different (bull and bear) market conditions; different valuation models (single and multi-index models); and compare this behaviour with that of a number of other transportation and non transportation industries within the US economy. The investigation is also extended at the international level to capture recent developments of the globalisation of the world economy and the formation of international industries operating beyond national borders.

According to Stopford (1997), the history of the water transportation industry since World War II has been one of ingenuity, professionalism, fabulous profits and some disastrous miscalculations. It involves the creation of "superstars" such as Niarchos and Onassis but also the occurrence of miscalculations such as the episode which took place in the tanker market in 1973 when orders were placed for over 100 million dwt of tankers, for which the demand never materialised. In short, as the aforementioned author rightly puts it, "shipping is an industry which is larger than life".

Adam Smith (1776), often regarded as the father of modern economics, described shipping as one of the major catalysts of economic development. In Chapter 3 of his famous book, The Wealth of Nations, he argued that shipping is a cheap source of transport which can open up wider markets to specialisation, offering shipment of even the most everyday products at prices far below those that can be achieved by any other means.

The first task of this chapter is to provide a brief analysis of the structure of the water transportation industry, with the discussion extended later to other industries analysed. In discussing the structure of this industry, one should be concerned with the way business is organised to achieve the efficient transport of different kinds of cargo. The major division

[1] The water transportation companies utilised for this purpose are presented in Appendix 2 of this chapter.

within the cargo carrying part of the industry is between bulk and liner shipping. The former specialises in the transport of large cargo parcels which can be carried on one ship one cargo basis. Thus, tramp ships travel on any sea-lane around the world in search of such cargoes to transport. Liner ships, on the other hand, specialise in the transportation of small cargo parcels, usually carried in containers. These ships provide regular services on specific sea-lanes around the world. Other segments of the water transportation industry include passenger vessels, ferries, tugs and other ancillary services, among others.

The bulk, liner and other segments of the water transportation industry have totally different approaches as far as the type of organisations involved and the respective shipping policies are concerned. For example, liner operators need to organise the transport of many different parcels and need a large shore - based staff, capable of dealing with shippers, handling documentation and planning the ship loading. Hence, due to their high overheads and also the need to maintain a regular service even when a full payload of cargo is not available, the liner business is vulnerable to uneconomic price competition from other shipowners operating on the same trade routes.

Contrary to that, the bulk shipping companies operate under the principle of "one ship - one cargo" and hence handle fewer, but much larger cargoes. Therefore, their operations do not require a large shore - based activity. Nevertheless, the few decisions that need to be made by a bulk shipping business are crucial and require the attention of the owner and/or vice - president. Large companies, shipping substantial quantities of bulk materials, often run their own shipping fleets to handle a proportion, or all, of their transport requirements. For example, according to Jacobs (1986), in 1984 the major oil companies collectively owned around 40% of the whole world tanker fleet. However, it should be stressed that industrial conglomerates do not necessarily become shipowners just to optimise the shipping operation. It is also to ensure that basic transport requirements are met at a predictable cost without the need to resort to the charter market.[2]

---

[2] The charter market occupies a central place in the structure of the shipping industry. Both shippers and shipping companies may prefer to hire a vessel rather than buy it outright. This may be due to the high capital cost of the vessel or the need to either cover cyclical peaks in demand for shipping capacity or replace ships out of service.

A major question throughout the years has been how to finance investments in this highly capital-intensive industry. Ships cost millions and such large sums need careful investment decisions. Methods of financing have varied over time and place, as well as with the corporate structure of the company requiring funds to invest in shipping. Thus, while traditional borrowing from banks (with owners offering equity as part financing in a mortgage) has always been prominent in the industry, charter backed finance (shipowners borrowing against the security of a long time charter agreement they have with a charterer) has been very popular in the post second world war period. This has been followed by asset backed finance in the 1980's (e.g. ship funds), and lately – in the 1990's - a lot of interest has been placed in drawing funds from the public. The latter may be materialised either by borrowing through the issuance of bonds, or by offering part-ownership to the public through shares in the company.

This book concentrates on this last form of finance of the industry. In particular, it concentrates on alternative valuation models of shares of water transportation companies trading in NY stock exchange. It examines single index models under which the market index alone is assumed to be driving market returns, and then extends this to multi index models as sets of micro economic and macroeconomic factors are considered as possible additional factors determining security returns. Security valuation models are also considered for stocks of other transportation industries and some other industries, listed in the same stock exchange in the US. International comparisons are also made by considering valuation issues through the formation of industries at the global level. This investigation enables comparisons of risk-return trade-offs between industries, a process which takes place by investors when taking practical investment decisions. The availability of listed companies in stock exchanges for each industry allows investors, by observing share price formation, to get a view of the market value of companies in each industry through the interplay of demand and supply forces driven by experts dealing in these stocks.

Despite the significance of the water and other transportation sectors in the US and the use of industry indices in investment decisions, there has been limited work in attempting to compare the risk - return performances of these industries (1) in a capital markets context and (2) in a comparative cross - industry context using asset pricing models. Equally limited attempts have been made to uncover factors, other than the market, that may influence returns in these industries. This might be due to the fact that since the seventies the sectors which provided superior returns to investors were, according to Jones (1993), the finance sector and, after the crash of 1987, the industrial sector. The exception to this lack of published work in the area is a series of studies by Kavussanos and Marcoulis (1995, 1997a,b,c, 1998, 2000a,b). While each of these publications provide answers separately to questions raised above, the pulling of these together in a single book, such as this one, helps to consider the issue of equity asset pricing and industry comparison in a unified way.

Thus, the analysis in this book would be revealing for investors in the water and other transportation industries, portfolio managers and corporate financiers since it can help them enhance investment decisions and perhaps induce investors to place a different share of their investment funds in these industries. Also, if one assumes that the market value of stocks in these industries reflects correctly the economic fundamentals prevailing in each industry (as evaluated by the experts dealing in these shares), and also that the companies listed in the stock exchange are representative of their industries, then conclusions may be drawn regarding the opportunity costs and prospects of investing in each of these economic sectors for business.

The second chapter of this book provides the background for understanding the technical terms used in the rest of the work. It is designed for readers who are interested in the exact methods used to derive results in subsequent parts of the book, and will enable them to replicate tests for their own research. The chapter can be omitted or read in a cursory manner and still be able to follow the results. It starts with a description of simple summary statistics of data and ways of evaluating significance of statistics like the mean and coefficients of skewness and kurtosis, among others. It continues with estimation methods of single and multi-equation regression models and inferences from such models. The concept of stationarity of time series and methods to test for them, as well as time series models are briefly outlined.

Chapter 3 describes the data used for the analysis in this book. It explains how the raw data on variables are obtained and what transformations of these variables are needed to produce the final series used for estimation in valuation models. The properties of these data are examined by considering relevant summary statistics, and some tentative conclusions are drawn in preparation for estimation of the final models in subsequent chapters.

The fourth chapter investigates the behaviour of water transportation company stock returns in the U.S. during the time period 1985 to 1994 in order to determine whether the systematic risk of this industry is different from that of the "average" company in the market, whether it has changed over the ten year period, over bull and bear market conditions, and whether there is a firm "size" effect in the industry. This chapter also undertakes a comparative analysis of the stock market perception of risk in U.S. listed water transportation companies and seven other major sectors: air transportation; rail transportation; trucks; electricity; gas; petroleum refining; and real estate, over an eleven year period (1984-1995). The industries utilised for this and the subsequent analyses have been selected due to their popularity among academics and practitioners and also due to them sharing some common characteristics with the water transportation industry. The analysis in this chapter has been carried out by employing the Capital Asset Pricing Model (CAPM) to model the stock returns of each industry and hence compare their betas (systematic risk).

The fifth chapter undertakes a multidimensional comparative analysis of the stock market perception of risk of U.S. listed water transportation and other transportation and non-transportation sectors. The set of microeconomic factors employed is: the market value of equity; the book - to - market value of equity ratio; the earnings - to - price ratio; the asset - to - market value of equity ratio; and the asset - to - book value of equity.

Chapter 6 is in the spirit of the fifth chapter, in the sense that it provides a multidimensional, multi - industry, analysis of the risk perception of the water transportation industry. However, the difference in this chapter is that a set of macroeconomic factors are utilised. This set comprises unanticipated changes in the following macroeconomic factors: industrial production; the term structure of interest rates; oil prices; consumption; and inflation.

The seventh chapter of the book combines the ideas of the fifth and sixth chapter to utilise both the set of microeconomic factors employed in chapter 5 and the set of macroeconomic factors employed in chapter 6 in a unified setting. It aims to identify and compare the determinants of the risk - return relationship of the water transportation industry against the other aforementioned industries.

Chapter 8 extends the analysis to an international setting. Today's transnational economy is also reflected in decisions made by portfolio managers in forming international portfolios of global industries. The chapter investigates the significance of a set of global macroeconomic factors in determining global industry returns. Morgan Stanley indices are readily available and enable such a comparison. Some interesting results emerge once one moves from the national to the international level.

Finally, chapter 9 provides a summary of the findings of the book. It discusses results for the transportation industries and other industries, under different model specifications, and provides a comparison between these. The findings are compared with other, similar, studies in the literature and similarities and differences are outlined. The usefulness of the findings for investors, portfolio managers and corporate financiers is also presented, which aims to provide ideas for practical implications of the results.

The rest of the current chapter is organised as follows. The next section outlines the analysis and selection procedure of common stocks in portfolio formation by investors. Section 1.3 reviews the voluminous literature dealing with the determinants of stock returns at the micro and macro economic level. Section 1.4 emphasises the importance of industry analysis and briefly mentions a number of studies dealing with industry stock returns comparisons. Section 1.5 describes the industry classification systems in the US paying particular attention to the Standard Industrial Classification (SIC) system, used in this book. Section 1.6 presents the industries utilised in this book and explains the rationale for selecting these industries. Finally, section 1.7 concludes the chapter.

1.2 The Decision Process for the Investor - Analysing and Selecting Stocks

This book focuses on understanding the determinants of stock returns, divided by industry, and utilising them in the stock selection procedure. This is done by dividing stocks according to their industrial classification and then identifying, and comparing, the determinants of returns at the microeconomic and macroeconomic level. A significant amount of research has been produced on the concept of efficient markets (see e.g. Fama(1991)), which has shaped the way academics and practitioners think about this issue. There are two well - known approaches to analysing and selecting stocks; fundamental and technical analysis. Traditionally, the former approach has dominated the majority of resources devoted to the analysis of common stocks and is concerned with the valuation of stocks according to fundamentals such as gearing ratios, book to market ratios, size and many more. Technical analysis deals with the search for identifiable and recurring stock price patterns and attempts to exploit market inefficiencies.

This book deals with fundamental analysis, the study of a stock's value using basic data at microeconomic and macroeconomic level. Fundamental analysis is based on the concept that any stock has an intrinsic value which is a multidimensional function of the general state of the economy (e.g. industrial production, inflation, oil prices etc.), the market, the structure of the industry the company operates in, and the company's fundamental microeconomic factors (e.g. capital structure, book - to - market ratio etc.).

It is important to start any analysis dealing with stocks by assessing the state of the economy which explicitly influences investors' everyday investment decisions. For example, if a recession is likely, or under way, stock prices will be heavily affected (they are likely to drop) at certain times during the contraction. Conversely, if a strong economic expansion is under way, stock prices will be heavily affected (they are likely to rise), again at particular times during the expansion. For instance, in 1997 when the world economy was performing exceptionally well, unprecedented rises were fuelled in stockmarkets all round the world.

Having completed an analysis of the economy an investment manager usually performs industry analysis. As we shall see in the next section, King (1966) was the first to present evidence that there is an industry factor affecting the variability in stock returns. Individual industries tend to respond to general market movements, but the degree of response can vary significantly due to the fact that industries undergo significant changes over both short and long periods of time. Furthermore, different industries are affected, to different degrees, by economic recessions and expansions. For example, the heavy goods industries will be severely affected in a recession (e.g. the auto and steel industries in the recession of 1981-1982). On the other hand, consumer goods industries might be much less affected during such a contractionary period.

Of course the opposite occurs when the economy is growing where income may be spent on investment or consumption goods. According to Begg, Fischer and Dornbusch (1987), when an increase in investment occurs, it raises income by a large amount (the investment multiplier), which in turn may produce an increase in demand for the product (the income accelerator) generating demand for more investment goods, so that the economic system expands rapidly. Eventually, labour and capital become fully utilised and the expansion is sharply halted, throwing the whole process into reverse.

During a severe inflationary period, such as the late seventies and early eighties, regulated industries, such as utilities, were severely hurt by their inability to pass along all price increases. Finally, from time to time, there appear to emerge new "hot" industries which enjoy spectacular growth. Examples that come to mind include genetic engineering and synthetic fuels and more recently dot.coms.

Once the investment manager has performed economy, market and industry analysis, he has to shift his emphasis on to company analysis. Security analysts focus on a number of factors which are important in analysing a company. These can be divided into two wide categories, qualitative factors and quantitative factors. Qualitative factors focus mainly on the managerial capacity of the company and its future prospects, which are fundamental to its success. Quantitative factors focus mainly on past and present income statements and the balance sheets of a company and include variables such as earnings, price - to - earnings multiples, dividend yields, capital structure, book - to - market ratios, size etc.

1.3 The Determinants of Stock Returns – General Literature Survey

Having briefly discussed the stock analysis and selection procedure in the previous section we focus next on the literature dealing with the determinants of stock returns at the microeconomic, company level, and at the macroeconomic level. The study of the determinants of stock returns has been a subject which has attracted the interest of academics, practitioners and investors for many years. Numerous academics have followed the example of King (1966) who is believed to be the first to study the determinants of stock returns. His study, utilising statistical methodologies of that time concluded that stock price changes could be expressed in terms of a market, an industry and a company effect. Effectively, what King proposed was that stock prices are shaped and determined by developments at the macroeconomic level, which in turn affect industries and the stock market in general, and by developments at the microeconomic level which affect the company's fundamentals, hence its value. King's findings were extremely important and were going to be the basis for a substantial amount of academic research which was to follow.

It is one of the aims of this first chapter of the book to briefly review the voluminous literature regarding the determinants of stock prices. One of King's findings, that of the market effect, was presented in a more formal way by Sharpe (1964) and Lintner (1965) and was to shape the way academics and practitioners perceived asset returns for a long time to come. The reference point is the Capital Asset Pricing Model (CAPM) which expresses the stock returns of any company as a linear function of just one factor, the return on the market portfolio of assets. The CAPM splits asset risk into two components, market or systematic risk, representing that portion of asset risk related to the riskiness of the market, and residual or non-systematic risk, which is unrelated to market movements. These ideas are summarised in equation (1.1).

$$R_{jt} = R_{ft} + \beta_j (R_{Mt} - R_{ft}) + \varepsilon_{jt} \qquad (1.1)$$

where R_{jt}, R_{ft}, R_{Mt} are the returns of company j, the risk - free rate and the market return, respectively, measured over time, t, β_j is a measure of market risk and ε_{jt} is the error term which captures residual risk.

However, during the late seventies and the early eighties, the discipline of finance and financial economics evolved and as computers became more powerful, a number of theoretical and practical criticisms regarding the validity of the CAPM arose. For example, Roll (1977) criticised the CAPM on the grounds that the composition, let alone the return, of the true market portfolio is not known to the researcher; what became widely known as the Roll Critique of the CAPM.

Others, such as Banz (1981), Basu (1977, 1983), Reinganum (1981), Lakonishok and Shapiro (1986), and Fama and French (1992), among others, observed that small firms appear to consistently earn higher returns than big firms, the well known "size effect". The economic rationale behind the "size effect" has been a puzzle and attempts have been made to explain it by arguing that (1) returns for small firms have been computed in a way that biases them upwards, (2) the risks on small firms have been understated, and (3) size may act as a proxy for some other economic influence.

Stattman (1980), Rosenberg, Reid and Lanstein (1985), Fama and French (1992), among others, found that there is a positive relationship between the average stock returns of US stocks and their ratio of book value of equity, BE, to market value of equity, ME. A similar relationship is documented for Japanese stocks by Chan, Hamao and Lakonishok (1991). Companies with a high BE/ME ratio are believed to be "value" stocks, while companies with a low BE/ME ratio are believed to be "growth" stocks. Generally speaking, "growth" stocks are stocks exhibiting rapid increases in earnings and that is why their market value of equity, reflecting their hypothetical excellent prospects, may be significantly higher than their book value of equity. On the other hand, "value" stocks are stocks whose market price seems to be low relative to their net worth. The empirical evidence suggests that "value" stocks seem to outperform "growth" stocks.

However, "value" and "growth" stocks may also be categorised by their earnings to price (E/P) ratio. Relatively low values of this ratio characterise "growth" stocks, while relatively high values characterise "value" stocks. Therefore, an interesting question that arises is whether there is any relationship between stock returns and their E/P ratios. Ball (1978), Reinganum (1981) and Basu (1983) argue that E/P ratios help to explain the cross - section of average returns on US stocks.

Another variable which has been the subject of empirical tests regarding the explanation of the cross - section of stock returns is leverage. Bhandari (1988) defined leverage as (Book Value of Total Assets minus Book Value of Equity)/(Market Value of Equity) and found that stock returns are positively related to market leverage. Fama and French (1992) included leverage, among a number of other variables, in an attempt to explain the cross - section of US stock returns and, in line with Bhandari (1988), found a positive relationship between market leverage, defined as the ratio of Total Assets/Market Value of Equity (A/ME) and stock returns. Furthermore, they defined book leverage as the ratio of Total Assets/Book Value of Equity (A/BE) and found a negative relationship between this ratio and stock returns.

An excellent discussion of the above determinants or "anomalies" of stock returns can be found in the seminal paper of Fama and French (1992), who employ a multifactor model to estimate the influence of the aforementioned factors on the cross - section of US stock returns.

The discussion so far has focused on a number of determinants of stock returns which, with the noticeable exception of the market, share a common characteristic, they all affect the company at the microeconomic level. An equally voluminous amount of literature exists with regards to macroeconomic factors which are also believed to have a role to play in the determination of stock returns. As in the case of the microeconomic factors, it is not possible to review all the papers dealing with macroeconomic factors and stock returns. However, an attempt will be made to review a number of the most important ones so as to obtain an insight of the role of the macroeconomy in the explanation of stock returns.

The effect of macroeconomic factors on stock returns can be thought to be a consequence of the pricing of stocks, as the stream of discounted expected future cash flows from holding a security. According to Damodaran (1994), the general stock valuation model is of the form presented in equation 1.2.

$$\text{Price of Security} = \sum_{t=1}^{t=\infty} \frac{DPS_t}{(1+r)^t} \tag{1.2}$$

where DPS_t denote expected dividends per share and r is the required rate of return on stocks.

It is clear from equation 1.2 that any macroeconomic factors which affects either the expectations of future cash flows to the investor (dividends per share) and/or the rate used to discount them will indirectly, though effectively, influence stock returns.

Chen, Roll and Ross (1986) were among the first to specify and test a set of economic factors which, based on economic theory and intuition, should affect stock returns either through future cash flows or through the discount rate. They utilised the following factors: inflation; the term structure of interest rates; risk premia and industrial production and found them to be significant in explaining stock returns. Although Chen, Roll and Ross (1986) can by no means claim that they have found the full set of variables for asset pricing they have most certainly made an important step in the right direction. Their model is of course an attempt to uncover factors, other than the market, influencing equity returns along the lines of the well-known Arbitrage Pricing Theory (APT).

Their work has been continued in a series of papers by Burmeister and McElroy(1987, 1988) who developed a multifactor model and found that five macroeconomic factors, similar, though not identical, to those employed by Chen, Roll and Ross (1986) are statistically significant in explaining stock returns. The factors they utilised were: default risk; the term structure of interest rates; inflation; sales as a proxy for the profits of the economy and; the market.

In the spirit of the above work, other researchers have studied the explanatory power of macroeconomic variables over stock returns in various stock exchanges across the world. For example, among others, Poon and Taylor (1991) applied the ideas discussed above to the UK, Martinez and Rubio (1989) applied them to the Spanish stock market, Hamao (1988) applied them to Japan and Wasserfallen (1989) applied them to a number of European countries. Most of the above studies find evidence in favour of the hypothesis that a set of macroeconomic factors has explanatory power over stock returns.

Chen and Jordan (1993), in a more recent study featuring the US market, employed a set of factors similar to the one used by Chen, Roll and Ross (1986) but grouped the companies in their sample according to their industry classification. The significance of industry groupings is something which will be discussed to a greater extent later on in this chapter. Nevertheless, Chen and Jordan (1993) also find evidence in favour of macroeconomic factors being significant in the pricing of stocks. More specifically, they document that, apart from the market returns, changes in oil prices and inflation are possible sources of risk.

However, as in the case of microeconomic factors, the study of macroeconomic factors and stock returns is not confined only to academics. Salomon Brothers (see Sorensen et al., 1989), better known today as Salomon Smith Barney, have developed a macroeconomic model in the spirit of the macroeconomic models we have been discussing above. This model uses seven variables to explain stock returns. They are: economic growth, measured by changes in industrial production; the business cycle, measured by the difference between corporate bonds and US Treasuries; long - term interest rates, measured by yield changes in the 10 - year Treasuries; short - term interest rates, measured by yield changes in the 1 - month Treasuries; inflation shock, measured by changes in the consumer price index; the US dollar, measured by changes in a 15 country currency basket Vs the dollar and; a market proxy. Salomon have been using their multifactor model for some time now and they claim that using monthly data, this model explains about 40% of the fluctuations in the returns of a sample of 1,000 stocks. Definitely then, models of this type are very promising.

In addition to the above, following their invention of the APT model, Roll and Ross created the Roll and Ross Asset Management Corporation to put their theory into practice. They begin by stating the systematic sources of risk that they believe are relevant to capital markets. These, according to the Roll and Ross Asset Management Corporation are: the business cycle; interest rates; investor confidence; short - term inflation and; long - term inflationary expectations (Sharpe, Alexander, and Bailey, 1995). Roll and Ross quantify these factors by designating certain macroeconomic variables as proxies. For example, the business cycle factor is represented by changes in the industrial production index. At the heart of the Roll and Ross approach lies the assumption that each source of risk is subjected to volatility and is entitled to some return. Moreover, Roll and Ross assume that individual securities and portfolios of securities possess different sensitivities to each source of risk. With these in mind, they construct investment portfolios which offer the most attractive risk - reward profile for the investor.

Another institution of international prominence which is dealing with multifactor models from a more practical angle is BARRA International. Their professionals utilise both fundamental (company specific) factors and macroeconomic factors to explain stock returns. For example, in 1993 BARRA International published a research paper (Engerman, 1993) whose aim was to compare a multifactor model utilising fundamental factors to another multifactor model utilising macroeconomic factors in the US. For the record, the fundamental factors were, the market; the stock's price momentum; size; trading activity; growth; the earnings - to - price ratio and; the book value - to - market value ratio. The macroeconomic factors were, interest rates; bond spreads; industrial growth; inflation; oil prices; gold price and; dollar's value. Their results indicate that both the microeconomic, fundamental, factors and the macroeconomic factors have a role to play in the explanation of stock returns. They, moreover, claim that microeconomic factors are more effective than macroeconomic factors in accounting for the cross - sectional variation in stock returns. In line with the above ideas, BARRA International is currently providing multifactor models for several countries including the US, Japan, the UK, Canada, France, Switzerland and many more. Reference to the BARRA models will be made again later in this chapter, when the importance of industry classification is discussed. Industry classification is indeed a prominent feature of the majority of BARRA's models.

1.4 Importance of the Industry Effect

1.4.1 A General Finance point of view

Having completed the discussion regarding the determinants of stock returns this section argues, from a general finance point of view, that there is scope to also include the industry classification variable in the analysis of stock returns. As discussed in the previous section, King (1966) was the first to argue that changes in stock prices can be explained by an industry effect as well as a market and a company effect. Also, Arditti (1967) and Nerlove (1968) find that industry differences are highly significant in explaining cross - sectional differences in stock price returns in the US stock market. Similar results are also produced in the industry focused analyses of Saunders and Yourougou (1990), Ferson and Harvey (1991) and Isimbabi (1994), among others. Hence, an investor whose aim is to build a diversified portfolio could well be interested in these cross - industry differences since he could utilise them to build a portfolio diversified across industries of different risk - return characteristics.

The importance of the industry effect is also emphasised in a number of other studies focusing on the US stock market. For example, Sorensen and Burke (1986) studied the relative price performance of several industry groups and concluded that an investment strategy based on buying and holding the best performing industry groups may enhance returns. Kane and Unal (1988) and Neuberger (1991) focused on the risk return characteristics of the US banking sector. They find banks to be greatly underpriced and exhibiting systematic risk that is lower than that of the "average" company. They also find that this systematic risk is increasing over time and that stocks of larger banks exhibit higher risk than small ones.

Gyourko and Keim (1993) focused on another "popular" US industry, real estate, and found that the average monthly returns of the industry are just under 1% with the associated standard deviation being over 7%. They then compared these figures with the corresponding figures of the S&P 500 index and found that the average monthly returns of the real estate industry are higher, but as might be expected are accompanied by higher standard deviation.

As in the previous section, the industry effect has not only been studied by academics. Prominent practitioners have also spent a lot of research time and resources to formulate models which encompass this effect. For example, BARRA International, who we introduced in section 1.3, very often estimates multifactor models for different industry groupings. One of their most widely used multiple - factor models, the BARRA E3 US model (Kahn, 1994), utilises microeconomic factors and estimates a model for each of 55 industry groups. Furthermore, their Canadian (Roy, 1992) and Japanese models (Rosenberg, 1991), both released in 1992, also utilise microeconomic and macroeconomic factors to estimate models across several industrial groupings.

Now, having reviewed some of the literature dealing with the industry effect, we return to our initial question of whether there is any scope for undertaking industry analysis and whether it pays to direct investment resources on to some industries at the expense of others at different points in time. We answer this question by considering some real world examples.

Table 1.1: Standard and Poor's Stock Price Indexes for Selected Industries

Industry	1941 -1943	1950	1973	1982	1986	1989
Aerospace	10	12	46	179	322	359
Broadcast Media				889	2255	5137
Capital Goods	10	18	119			
Chemicals				57	32	41
Computer and Business Equipment	10	20	1450	1412	2032	N/A.
Copper				55	52	N/A.
Drugs	10	14	245	248	540	967
Electronics	10	23	685			
Gold Mining	10	10	64			
Lead and Zinc	10	12	17			
Oil Well Equipment and Service	10	22	145	1312	999	1702
S&P 400 Industrial Average	10	18	121	156	270	N/A.
Shoes				108	149	323
Steel				32	28	51
Sugar	10	16	30			
Textile Apparel	10	13	31	63	174	198

Source: Jones (1993), Investments: Analysis and Management, 4th Edition, John Wiley & Sons Inc.
Notes: 1. Base 1941 - 1943 = 10, 2. N/A. = Not Available

As might be observed in table 1.1 (Jones, 1993), over the 30 year period 1943-1973, the computer and business equipment industry did extremely well (145 times what it was in 1941) thanks primarily to IBM, (even without IBM, this industry would still have been 43 times larger than its base). The electronics industry also did well, rising to almost 69 times its 1941 level. On the other hand, the lead and zinc industry was less than twice its original level, and the sugar and textile apparel industries were only three times their original levels. Over shorter periods of time, industries also tend to perform differently. For example, during the fifties the price index for the electronics industry increased almost tenfold, whereas that of the textile apparel industry increased only twofold.

Moving on with some more examples from the eighties we also witness tremendous differences among industries' performances as measured by the Standard and Poor's (S&P) Stock Price Industrial Indexes. During the period 1982-1989, the drugs industry almost quadrupled, the broadcast media industry rose to almost six times its 1982 level while on the other hand the chemicals industry declined by almost 30%.

Table 1.2: Standard and Poor's Industry Groups with the Best and Worse Performance during the Market Crash of 1987

Best Performers		Worst Performers	
Electric Companies	-3,50%	Toys	-41,80%
Telephone	-8,10%	Machine Tools	-41,30%
Property/Casualty Insurers	-14%	Leisure Time	-40,30%
Beverage-Brewers	-14,60%	Miscellaneous Metals	-39,40%
International Oils	-14,70%	Gold	-38,30%
Household Products	-15,20%	Offshore Drilling	-38%
Multi - Line Insurance	-15,30%	Auto Trucks and Parts	-36,80%
Diversified Health Care	-15,90%	Chapter Containers	-35%
Beverage- Soft Drinks	-16,30%	Electronics-Semiconductors	-33,90%
Food Companies	-17,20%	Tires and Rubber Goods	-33,80%
Drug Companies	-17,40%	Manufactured Housing	-33,20%
Medical Products, Suppliers	-18,40%	Miscellaneous Financial	-32,70%
Restaurants	-18,80%	Aluminium	-32,60%
Computer Software, Services	-18,90%	Retail Department Stores	-32,10%
		Home-building	-31,80%
S&P 500	-21,80%		
Dow Jones Industrials	-23,20%		

Measured between 30/9/1987 and 30/10/1987.
Source: Jones (1993), Investments: Analysis and Management, 4th Edition, John Wiley & Sons Inc.

However, the most dramatic example during the period mentioned is that produced by the market crash of October 1987 when the Dow Jones Industrials index lost 23.2%. Industries such as toys, machine tools, leisure time, gold, and offshore drilling, among others, lost around 40% of their value while others such as electric companies and telephone companies lost less than 10%. Table 1.2 (Jones, 1993) clearly demonstrates that the losses suffered by investors varied widely according to the particular industries held.

From the evidence depicted above, one can conclude that it would have been beneficial for an investor to have performed careful industry analysis at any point in time, from the post - war period to date.

1.4.2 A Strategy point of view

Having established that there is significant variability in industry attractiveness as evidenced through differing stock returns and risks, over time we consider the issue next from a strategy point of view. Before embarking on this task, it is essential to distinguish between two activities in the strategic analysis of any business: the formulation of the business strategy and the valuation of the business strategy. The former typically entails analysing the attractiveness of the industry and the position of the company vis - a - vis its competitors while the latter is concerned with the estimation of the shareholder value added by alternative strategies. This process may be depicted in figure 1.1.

Figure 1.1: Strategy Formulation and Valuation Process

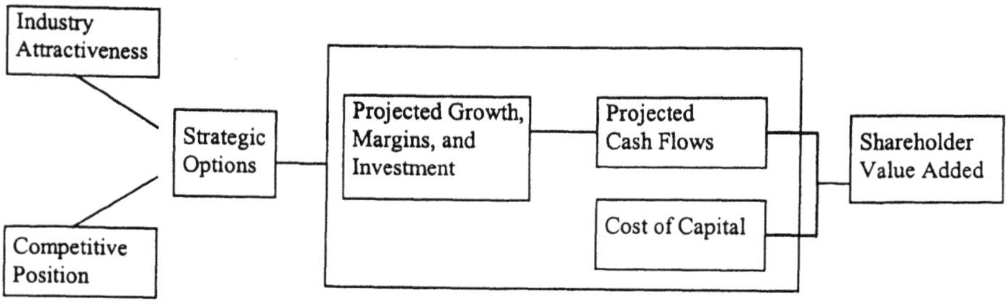

Perhaps no framework has had greater influence on management thinking and acting than the one developed by Michael Porter in his seminal work, Competitive Strategy

(Porter, 1980). Porter focuses on industry attractiveness, among a number of other factors such as a company's competitive position within the industry and its sources of competitive advantage.

The fundamental purpose of industry attractiveness analysis, they argue, is to gauge the value creation potential of each of the industries included in the investment set of the investor or the fund manager. This analysis should provide, among other things, answers to the following questions:

- How attractive is the industry?
- How would likely changes in market characteristics or industry structure alter industry attractiveness?
- What resources and capabilities are critical for creating value in the industry today and in a changed future environment?

To identify how attractive an industry is likely to be, market characteristics and the industry's structure must be examined. Market characteristics that need to be analysed include the expected growth in the market, supply and demand characteristics for the customers and the suppliers, technological change, regulatory change, and other environmental issues. Factors affecting industry structures that warrant addressing include the distribution of market share, entry and exit barriers, vertical integration potential, threat of substitute products, modes of competition and industry profitability.

The attractiveness of an industry will also be affected by the level of investment in resources and capabilities required sustaining its value creating potential. The level of investment in human and physical capital will not only affect the overall profitability of the industry, but also its competitive structure. For example, a high level of required investment coupled with hard - to - differentiate products or services will likely lead to consolidation in an industry.

For the purposes of this short discussion, it is important to establish that the economic forces governing industry attractiveness ultimately impact upon shareholder returns because they influence prices, quantities sold, costs, investments, and the overall riskiness of companies in the industry. These variables, in turn, are the building blocks for the value driver determinants of shareholder value. Specifically, sales growth is determined by price and quantity; and operating profit margin is determined by costs relative to prices and quantities sold. Investment conventionally comprises two essential value drivers: working capital and fixed capital investment. However, we should note that in recent years "expensed knowledge investments", that is investments in highly specialised human resources, have become the largest and most critical investments in many industries. Finally, risk is conditioned by an industry's business risk and financial risk.

1.5 Industry Classification of Industries

Having deduced that the industry factor is important in the analysis of stock returns, we discuss how industries are classified in practice. At first glance, the term industry may appear to be self - explanatory. After all, most of us are familiar with the auto industry, the drug industry, the electric utility industry and so forth. But, are these classifications as clear-cut as they seem? The answer is no and therefore, in order for the aforementioned analysis to be able to be implemented, the analyst and the investor need a method, or a system, with which to classify industries.

SIC classifies companies into industries according to their final product or service.

Table 1.3: The 11 Major Divisions of the SIC System

Division A	Agriculture, Forestry, and Fishing
Division B	Mining
Division C	Construction
Division D	Manufacturing
Division E	Transportation
Division F	Wholesale Trade
Division G	Retail Trade
Division H	Finance, Insurance and Real Estate
Division I	Services
Division J	Public Administration
Division K	Non- classifiable Establishments

The best known and most widely used system is the Standard Industrial Classification (SIC) System which is based on Census data and classifies companies into industries according to their final product or service.[3] SIC codes have 11 letter divisions, A to K (see Table 1.3) and each division consists of several major industry groups, designated by a two digit numerical code. The major industry groups, within each division, are further subdivided into three, four, and five - digit SIC codes to provide even more detailed classifications. Clearly, the larger the number of digits in the SIC system, the more specific the breakdown.

Figure 1.2 depicts how the system moves along digits and provides more detail. For example, let us consider division E, the transportation division. This consists of 10 major groups as per 2-digit number; 40, 41,...,49. Major group 44 corresponds to water transportation which consists of six further 3 digit groupings. Grouping 441 refers to deep-sea foreign transportation of freight, which only has one four-digit category under it. In the case of other categories, the breakdown may reach, as already mentioned, 5 digit groupings.

Figure 1.2: Example of the SIC System - Division E

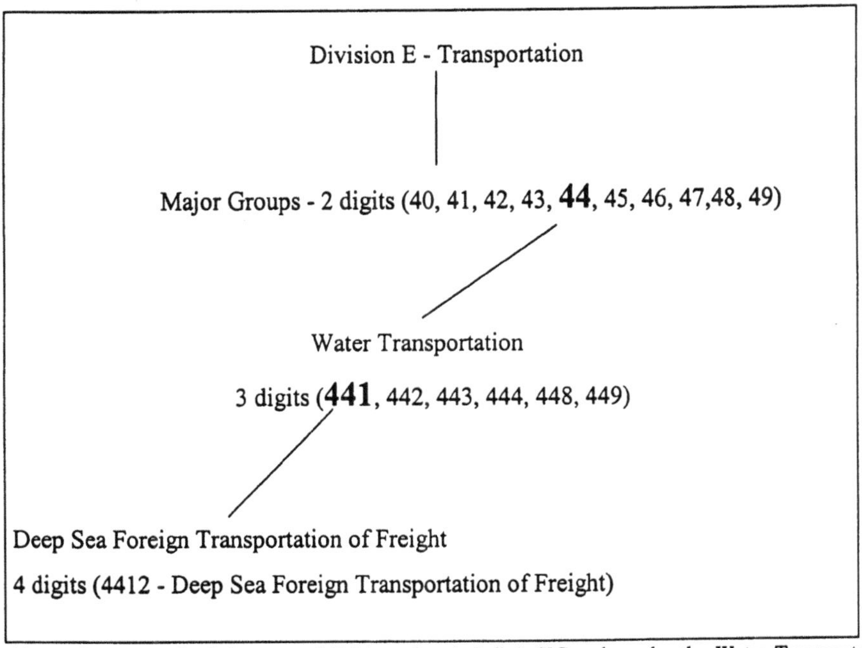

Notes: See Appendix 1 for exact definition of each 3-digit SIC code under the Water Transportation industry group. In the same appendix, also, there are details of the SIC codes for the other industry groups examined in this book (e.g. 40 for Railroad Transport and 45 for Air Transportation).

[3] See census of Manufacturers (Washington DC: U.S. Government Printing Office).

SIC codes have significantly contributed towards bringing order to the industry classification problem by providing a consistent basis for describing industries and companies. Analysts using SIC codes can focus on economic activity in as broad, or as specific, a manner as desired. For example, industry groupings in a number of studies dealing with industry stock return comparisons in the U.S. (e.g. Ferson and Harvey, 1991, Eun and Resnick, 1992, Isimbabi, 1994, and Boudoukh, Richardson and Whitelaw, 1994), among others, have been formulated according to their SIC codes. Typically, the above studies have used 2 - 4 digit industry groupings.

Despite the fact that the SIC system of industry classification is the easiest to use and the most consistent system available, it is not the only one in actual use. Standard and Poor's Corporation, as from the end of 1982, provide weekly stock indices on approximately 100 industry groupings, many of which go back 30 or even 40 years. The Value Line Investment Survey covers roughly 1,700 companies, divided into approximately 90 industries. Moreover, another useful industry classification system is that of The Media General Financial Weekly which divides stocks into 60 industries.

Given its many advantages and its wide use among academics and practitioners the SIC classification system is used in this book. Nonetheless, like any classification system, it faces certain limitations, the most important of which is the classification of multiproduct, diversified companies under more than one heading. When we perform cross industry comparison later in the book, in order to avoid distorting the results during comparisons between the selected industries, companies that were found to be listed under more than one industry groups have been omitted. This results in industry groupings which are relatively homogeneous. The names of the companies which remain listed under each industry, as a result of these omissions, are shown in appendix 2 of this chapter.

1.6 Industries Used for the Purposes of this Book

1.6.1 US Transportation Industries

Transportation in the US is nowadays available in four distinct modes: air, sea, rail, and truck. In the past, each transportation mode operated independently of the others, in classic "stovepipe" fashion. Shipments that required the use of more than one mode were considered multimodal, but each leg of the trip was considered an individual shipment, with the shipper usually negotiating and co-ordinating. Competition within the transportation industry and today's dynamic, global business environment have led to the increased use of a new transportation strategy, known as intermodalism, which seeks to minimise the seams in the transportation process in order to streamline movements, increase reliability, and reduce costs.

Since our analysis focuses on US transportation stocks, it is now appropriate to briefly take stock of the current conditions pertaining in the aforementioned US transportation sectors:

Water Transportation:
The U.S.-flagged deep-sea intermodal shipping industry carries merchandise between the U.S. and foreign ports in direct connection with other merchant vessels in the world fleet. Strategic in nature, it is interconnected to the domestic segments of air, rail, and trucking at seaports. By nature, waterborne shipping is particularly suited for the movement of heavy, bulky, and low-value-per-unit commodities for which speed is not of primary importance.

According to the Transportation Industry Study Report (1996), the U.S. share of the global ocean-going shipping industry continues to be small. In 1993, only 17.0 million tons (16.2 percent) of a worldwide total of 104.8 million tons of commercial liner cargo was carried on U.S.-flagged vessels. In 1984 the U.S. total was 13.8 million tons, or 21.7 percent. The total value of liner cargo carried in 1993 was $344.7 billion, with U.S.-flagged vessels transporting $69.2 billion worth, or 20.1 percent of the total; in 1984 the U.S. share was $41.2 billion. The net earnings of the entire U.S.-flagged foreign-trade liner fleet were only $119 million in 1992.

According to the same report, in 1985, the U.S.-flagged fleet numbered 477 ships. By 1994, that number had dropped to 332 U.S.-flagged vessels actively engaged in commerce: 27 break-bulk cargo ships, 129 intermodal vessels, 154 tankers, and 20 bulk carriers. Since 1994, 30 U.S.-flagged vessels have either been scrapped as inefficient or reflagged to a flag-of-convenience.

So despite the fact that the United States has the world's most extensive system of both deep-water and inland ports and harbours, and it is still the world's largest maritime trading nation, today, according to the Transportation Industry Study Report (1996), 97% of all cargoes by water to and from American ports and foreign ports sail on foreign flag vessels. These include 307 foreign-flagged vessels owned by U.S. citizens, or corporations, which, like all foreign-flagged vessels, are subject to the laws of the foreign country whose flag they fly, not the laws to which U.S-flag vessels are subject.

According to The Jones Act Reform Coalition Report (1998), a primary reason for the above phenomenon has been The Jones Act which, since 1920, essentially requires that all goods shipped by water from one port in the US to another - including trade between the East and West Coasts, the Gulf region, the Great Lakes and the non-contiguous states and territories - must be: (1) carried on vessels built and documented (flagged) in the United States; (2) manned with American crews; and (3) owned and operated by American citizens.

These restrictions are referred to as cabotage laws, and they have been almost totally repealed in the remaining industrialised countries of the world in the broad extent to which they are applied in the United States. According to the aforementioned report, only three countries, Brazil, Indonesia, and Peru, have maritime cabotage laws as extensive and restrictive as those of the United States.

The water transportation industry is the last bastion of heavy federal regulation of transportation in the US. The maritime deregulation legislation, currently before Congress, contains several elements that may result in more competition for available freight and a consolidation of major carriers. As in the now-deregulated air transportation industry, this increased competition will encourage the emergence of new global transportation alliances that will allow ocean carriers to share not only assets, such as vessels, but also container equipment and terminal facilities.

According to the Transportation Industry Study Report (1996), another great challenge facing today's U.S. merchant marine fleet is the ongoing debate over the role of subsidies in maintaining an adequate U.S. capability to meet national defence needs. U.S. mobility plans rely heavily on the U.S.-owned merchant fleet for the sustainment of U.S. forces deployed overseas, and subsidies have been considered a cost-effective means of ensuring that military-useful vessels, primarily container and a small number of roll-on/roll-off (RO/RO) ships, are available. The Operating Differential Subsidy (ODS), which expired in 1997, offset higher costs associated with all-U.S.-citizen mariner crews. The new subsidy program, the Maritime Security Act of 1995, would provide approximately $2 million per ship for 50 U.S.-flagged ships, but is currently stalled in the Senate. Proponents argue that the subsidy is necessary to guarantee that U.S.-flagged and -operated shipping is available to ensure support in a contingency. Opponents believe that the 10-year program's $1 billion price tag is too steep and that U.S. cabotage laws (the Jones Act) and government cargo preferences adequately support sufficient sustainment capacity in the U.S.-flagged fleet. Subsidy opponents also note that U.S. shipping that does reflag will remain under effective U.S. control and will continue to be available to meet defence needs. Subsidy programs must be balanced against the need for other maritime programs, such as the procurement of additional surge RO/ROs, large, medium-speed RO/ROs (LMSRs) and afloat pre-positioning vessels for the U.S. Ready Reserve Force (RRF). The RRF was created to maintain a surge shipping and re-supply capability that would be available on short notice to support the development of a multi-division force.

Air Transportation:

The United States may be characterised as a truly air - oriented nation. This is epitomised by the fact that it contains more airports than the entire rest of the world, serviced by a large number of air carriers. Additionally it should be noted that according to the Transportation Industry Study Report (1996), over 184,000 aircraft are registered in the US and 6 of the top 10 airlines in the world are of U.S. identity.

According to the aforementioned study, air transport is the "premium" way to move people and cargo since it is both the fastest and most expensive mode. For most air carriers, passenger revenues account for the vast majority of income, with cargo (at 4-6% of revenues) of much less significance. Nevertheless, although air transport is very often described as the most efficient means of transporting people, it cannot compete with other modes, such as water transportation, in transporting low - value, high - bulk cargo. Therefore, most airfreight is high - value, time - sensitive material. Nowadays, air carriers specialising in overnight, express, and small - package deliveries, such as Federal Express, United Parcel Service (UPS), and DHL, account for more than 50 percent of domestic air freight.

Financially, according to the Air Industry Overview (1995), the industry suffered huge losses for the early part of the nineties but, in 1995, it reported record profits of $5.3 billion. As a result, airline stocks soared by over 46 percent. However, according to the same overview, the latest Department of Transportation (DOT) statistics show that revenue passenger - miles exceeded 500 million, an increase of almost 90 percent over the past 15 years while revenue ton - miles of freight exceeded 22 million, an increase of 125 percent since 1980.

The same publication also indicates that the DOT and the Air Transport Association project that the record - breaking profits posted by the U.S. airlines in 1995 will continue for the foreseeable future, with the majority of the industry's growth taking place internationally. This shift in market emphasis has generated an increasing number of alliances and mergers between domestic and foreign carriers. Yet the continued health of the air transportation industry remains closely tied to the overall U.S. economy, since 90 percent of airline profits are derived from passenger travel, and half of that figure is derived from business travel.

Increased competition in the industry, brought about by deregulation since 1978, has forced some less competitive and less viable air carriers to close their doors and others to merge in order to stay viable. Stiff competition will continue to force closures and mergers in the future. The main challenges facing the domestic airline industry include international access and competition, government policies and requirements, and infrastructure and prime equipment requirements for the next century. Airlines are faced with huge capital investment requirements if they are to maintain state-of-the-art aircraft in their fleets. Older aircraft are less fuel efficient and grow increasingly expensive to operate and maintain. New, replacement aircraft have smaller crew requirements and more quiet, fuel efficient engines, but purchase prices can easily exceed $100 million. And those carriers fortunate enough to be able to procure new aircraft are faced with a shrinking number of commercial aircraft suppliers.

A relatively new feature in the industry is globalization of airlines. According to the Transportation Industry Study Report (1996), a 1995 General Accounting Office report stated that existing bilateral pacts between the United States and 72 other nations greatly restricted the airlines' ability to participate in foreign markets. The result is that more and more carriers have entered into code-sharing agreements whereby U.S. and foreign carriers agree to share flight numbers, passengers, and even equipment to ensure access to international markets. Since 1992, the number of code-sharing agreements has increased from 19 to 61. Three of these alliances, namely Northwest/KLM, USAir/British Airways, and United/Lufthansa, are considered "strategic" since they affect key routes and assets. Industry analysts fear that the continued growth of code-sharing agreements could result in decreased competition as large, multicarrier alliances deny market access to non-alliance members. Code sharing could also have a negative affect on U.S. national security. If domestic carriers become too reliant upon code sharing for access into international markets, they will be less inclined to purchase and maintain large, wide-body aircraft for international overseas flights. Without these aircraft in their inventories, domestic carriers will be unable to adequately support Department of Defense (DoD) mobilization requirements.

Rail Transportation:

Despite the fact that railroads have been moving freight and passengers in the US for over 165 years, according to the Transportation Industry Study Report (1996), motor vehicles and aeroplanes have nowadays made passenger trains unprofitable and nearly obsolete. Therefore, modern U.S. railroading is focused on long - haul, heavy cargo movements which include the transportation of commodities such as coal and grain as well as the transportation of intermodal containers, motor vehicles and other heavy equipment.

Despite the fact that in the 60s and 70s, transportation pundits predicted that the U.S. railroad industry was in its death throes due to its obsolete infrastructure and strongly unionised labour force, the railroad industry managed to survive and today it is strong once again. In 1994, according to Rail Industry Overview (1995), for example, 1.2 million revenue ton - miles, nearly 40 percent of US freight, were carried by the railroad industry for an annual revenue of over $33 billion. This profitability was reflected in Standard & Poor's rail stock index, which grew 198 percent between 1987 and 1994.

A major reason for the railroad industry's turnaround was the consolidation of railroad companies through acquisitions and mergers. Indicatively, it should be noted that today, according to the Transportation Industry Study Report (1996), only 10 Class I railroads (those with revenues over $255.8 million) remain in the United States, down from 40 in 1979. This dramatic concentration is also seen in terms of the industry's market - share breakdown. In 1974, the 5 largest U.S. railroads earned only 40 percent of total railroad revenue while in 1994 the top 5 railroads accounted for 85 percent of industry revenue. The consolidated railroads have been able to enjoy several of the theoretical advantages stemming from merger and acquisition activity such as the elimination of duplicated overheads, the withdrawal of unproductive lines, the updating of infrastructure and equipment and the better utilisation of labour resources. In addition to the above, deregulation has allowed them to get out of unprofitable business sectors and focus on what railroads do best which is simply to move freight over long distances.

Trucks:

The trucking industry moves products from one point to another using either hired carriers, in which case the transport freight belongs to others, or private carriers which are operated by individual manufacturers, wholesalers, and merchants for delivery of their own goods. According to the Transportation Industry Study Report (1996), the number of trucks on U.S. roads has grown rapidly over the past few years, reaching over 45 million registered trucks in 1992 and the number of new trucks added to the fleet every year has remained steady at 8 - 10 percent, indicating a healthy replacement rate as trucks stay in service for about 10 - 12 years. It should also be noted that today, over 5 million Americans are employed in truck - related occupations.

The industry may be decomposed into general freight carriers which generate the majority of all truck revenues and specialised carriers thus include carriers which typically carry heavy machinery, liquid petroleum, refrigerated products, agricultural commodities, motor vehicles, building materials and household goods.

Like the airline industry, trucks are considered to be a strategic industry which offers flexibility and versatility. As a result, an efficient motor carrier can, on the one hand, compete with an air carrier on point - to - point service for a shipment of any size for distances of less than 500 miles, while, on the other hand, for distances which exceed 500 miles, trucks can easily compete with rail carriers for truckload - sized shipments. Moreover, since the present intermodal infrastructure is not fully capable of seamless rail - sea, rail - air, or air - sea connectivity, trucks usually fill the seams and function as the linchpins of the intermodal process. In terms of productivity, according to the Trucking Industry Market Data Book (1995), freight movement by trucks has increased by 60 percent since the 1980s, to over 880,000 million ton - miles in 1993. Subsequently, the total revenue of the trucking industry increased by 87 percent over the same period to over $292 billion in 1992.

1.6.2 Non - Transportation Industries

Electricity:

According to Thierer (1997), America's electricity market employs total assets worth approximately $500 billion and generates net revenues of over $200 billion per annum. The size of this market is not surprising, considering that almost every American is a consumer of electricity. Despite the fact that millions purchase and use electricity, few have a choice in deciding from whom they will receive their service. And, according to the same author, a confusing set of outdated, inefficient, and overlapping laws and regulations continue to govern the electricity industry at the federal, state, and local levels.

However, the way Americans buy electricity appears to be changing since advances in technology, combined with pressures to reduce prices, are transforming the industry from one comprised of monopolistic, turf-bound utilities to one featuring more competitive firms vying for customers across state lines. In many ways, the industry is responding to the same forces that transformed the banking, telecommunications, and airlines industries just a few years ago.

Even though electricity is one of the most commonly consumed goods or services in the developed world, few understand how it is produced, how it is delivered where it is needed, and how the prices paid for it are determined. To understand the implications of future changes, one needs to take a quick look at the present situation.

According to the Resources for the Future (1997), today, the U.S. electricity industry has a vertical shape. Typically, a single company in a given geographic area generates electricity, transmits it to cities and towns, and then downloads and distributes power to factories, businesses, and homes. The industry's three functions are power generation, long-distance transmission, and local distribution and they have long been regarded as "natural monopolies." Keeping costs low has meant relying on one entity, usually an electric utility, to provide all three functions. Thus, although electricity is a top item of consumption, consumers, whether commercial, industrial, or residential, have had little say in its purchase. Now, however, the old monopolies are coming apart. Generating electricity has become viable as a competitive enterprise. New high-efficiency gas turbines and combined-cycle gas turbines that generate electricity have lower combined capital and operating costs than traditional generators. Consequently, small, modularised systems can be manufactured to generate electricity at the same low cost as that from very large central power stations built only a few decades ago. Moreover, these new, smaller units are mobile, and can be shipped and plugged into existing transmission systems that deliver electricity to towns or to a single unit, such as a factory.

According to Resources for the Future (1997), it is the economic savings arising from these new technologies in generation that is changing the "look" of the electricity industry. By reducing the size of generating plants, electricity generation can now be "unbundled" from transmission and distribution, the other two functions that traditionally were monopolised and provided as a package deal.

At the same time that technological advances have begun to chip away at old ways, the tradition of basing electricity prices on costs has come under increasing criticism. Closely regulated local utilities, each enjoying a government-protected franchise territory and the luxury of setting prices based on costs, have felt little pressure to adapt or expand their service offerings to meet changing customer needs. Cost-based prices give utilities little incentive to run lean operations, since their revenues and profits would take a corresponding hit through lower prices.

Cost-based pricing also means that prices dip and peak even among closely located utilities, depending on local fuel rates and other variables. Prices yo-yo across the continent of franchised territories that each utility dominates. According to the same author, in many high-rate states in the Northeast and in California, you may pay 50 percent above the national average. As of September 1996 consumers in the State of New York were paying the highest residential price for electricity at about 14.7 cents per kilowatt-hour. At the other end of the spectrum consumers in the State of Washington were paying about 5.0 cents per hour.

Competition provides a remedy to these disparities. Proposals to deregulate electricity generation and expand competitive electric power markets have been adopted by some states and are under consideration by many others. Some analysts argue that the benefits of efficient, low-cost, and high-quality electricity service can be had even without consumer participation. What is needed, they say, is for states to adopt methods that give utilities incentives to reduce their costs. Other observers argue, however, that only if consumers enter directly into the market will the full benefits of competition be realised. The lines of debate are largely set by opposing views of the outcome of each of these two scenarios.

The potential benefits of bringing more competition into the electricity industry, lower prices, reduced production costs, more services, ultimately will depend on how competition is put into effect. Although otherwise quite varied, proposals now under consideration are based on two distinct approaches: expanded wholesale competition and the introduction of competition at the retail level.

Petroleum Refining:

Petroleum refining deals with the separation of crude oil into its major distillation fractions which are then further processed into finished petroleum products. These fall into three major categories: fuels (e.g. motor gasoline, diesel and distillate fuel oil, liquefied petroleum gas); finished non-fuel products (e.g. solvents, lubricating oils, petroleum wax); and chemical industry feedstocks (e.g. naphtha, ethane, propane). These petroleum products according to the National Energy Policy Plan (1995), comprise about 40 percent of the total energy consumed in the U.S. and are used as a primary input to a vast number of products such as fertilisers, pesticides, paints, waxes, thinners, solvents etc. According to the same source this market share is likely to remain constant in the coming decade or so.

Generally speaking, the US petroleum refining industry can be characterised by a relatively small number of large operators which, for reasons of efficiency in transporting crude oil feed stocks and finished products, are sited near crude oil sources such as onshore petroleum terminals and oil and gas extraction areas or consumers such as heavily industrialised areas. Consequently, the distribution of facilities is more concentrated along the Gulf Coast and near the heavily industrialised areas of both east and west coasts.

The petroleum refining industry in the US has felt considerable economic pressures in the past decade arising from a number of factors such as increased costs of labour and compliance with new safety and environmental regulations. A rationalisation period began after crude oil pricing and entitlements were decontrolled in early 1981 and as a result of that, market forces determined that there was surplus capacity and margins dropped to facilitate the closure of the least efficient capacity. However, despite the closing of refineries, total output of finished products has remained relatively steady with slight increases in the past two years. These were due to the increased capacity and utilisation rates of existing facilities.

Recent and future environmental and safety regulatory changes are expected to force the petroleum refining industry to make further substantial investments in upgrading certain refinery processes to reduce emissions and alter product compositions. This is likely to result, firstly, in increasing prices of petroleum products which in turn implies little, if any, increase in the demand for refined petroleum products in the near future and, secondly, the closure of more refineries.

Gas:

According to National Energy Policy Plan (1995), the use of gas and especially natural gas, is today a major source of energy in the US, providing about 25 percent of all energy used in the country. The gas industry has increased by 35 percent over the last decade and now serves about 60 million customers and employs more than 170,000 people. As a result of the industry's strong fundamentals and growth, stocks of natural gas companies have had a significant increase in value during the past few years.

Moreover, the industry appears to be favoured by environmentalists since it is believed that the increased use of natural gas addresses several environmental concerns simultaneously, including smog, acid rain and greenhouse gas emissions. In addition to its environmental appeal, natural gas is inherently efficient since about 90 percent of the gas produced is delivered to the customer as usable energy.

Given the above, along with the continued strong industrial demand and the popularity of gas among new - home buyers and commercial customers, one can expect further substantial growth in US gas consumption, market share and production in the future. The strongest growth is expected to take place in the electric utility sector, where the economic and environmental benefits of gas - fired generation will enable gas to continue capturing the lion's share of the market for new generating capacity. Having said that, it is important to note that the actual growth of the industry is likely to be subjected to variables such as weather conditions, economic growth rates and oil prices which are, to a large extent, exogenously determined.

Real Estate:

According to Sharpe, Alexander and Bailey (1995), the real estate industry provides attractive investment opportunities for most investors due to the fact that it offers long-lived assets with steady cash flow schedules and a huge diversified market. The returns on real estate, according to the same source, tend to exhibit relatively low correlations with those of stocks and bonds, and a positive correlation with inflation.

The above reasons explain why the real estate industry has traditionally been considered to be a must-own investment and a prerequisite for asset diversification purposes and inflation hedging. As a result, there was a point in time when the real estate industry was worth more than all the securities that were traded on the New York, American, and over-the-counter Exchanges and was not affected by regulations, codes, and environmental issues. Sadly, for the industry, these advantages no longer exist and the industry has to compete for investment capital on an equal footing with other types of businesses; bottom line to bottom line, prospects to prospects, value to value.

Historically, according to Simanoff (1998), the real estate industry can be characterised as a cyclical industry much affected by external macroeconomic factors. The industry experienced a boom in the late seventies which began busting in 1979 when the Federal Reserve began making sharp increases in the prime lending rate to control inflation. Following that, and although financing was readily available for real estate development, high interest rates and a slow-moving economy brought the industry to a halt. By 1983, however, interest rates were moving down rapidly as the US entered a 15-year period of low inflation and what followed over the next seven years was the greatest real estate boom ever witnessed. Nevertheless, as might be expected of a cyclical industry, in 1991 - as in 1979 - the real estate industry collapsed, this time due to an overheated economy and what was to become known as the "savings and loan crisis". This collapse was the worst real estate depression in US modern history.

Today, the industry has recovered to a point at which there are space shortages. Demand is strongly outpacing supply and the industry is looking warily at the current burst of growth and is wondering what it can expect in the 21st century. However, it should be noted that it is not likely that we will witness the excess overbuilding of space we did in the prior two booms since underwriting criteria appear to be higher.

1.6.3 Rationale for selecting the above Industries

At the core of this book lies the behaviour of US listed water transportation stocks and their comparison with that of transportation and a number of, other, non-transportation industries. The rationale for the selection of the industries chosen is purely intuitive and aims at providing the reader with meaningful comparisons. More specifically, the air transportation, rail transportation and trucks industries have been chosen due to the fact that they are transportation industries. Hence, they might be argued to compete, in one way or another, with the water transportation industry in the investor's stock selection decision. At the same time, inclusion of every transportation sector in the analysis extends the scope of the book to make it of wider interest to parties interested in all transportation industries.

The petroleum refining, electricity and gas industries were chosen due to their stable growth nature which is directly opposite to the very cyclical nature of the water transportation industry[4]. Finally, the real estate industry has been included due to its cyclical nature which, as already mentioned, is a characteristic of the water transportation industry as well. In addition to the above, it should also be noted that the four non-transportation industries have been selected due to the fact that they have been, over the years, popular with academics focusing on industry comparisons. For example, Isimbabi (1994) undertook a comparative analysis of the stock market perception of banks and compared it with that of other industries including gas, electricity and petroleum refining.

Now, having briefly discussed the rationale behind the selection of the particular industries utilised in this book, it is appropriate to focus on the water transportation industry more extensively. The listing of water transportation companies in the United States is a relatively new phenomenon, with most companies entering the stock exchange to raise funds in the last couple of decades. It is worth noting that currently,

[4] Taken from HSBC James Capel which uses three categories to analyse stocks, stable growth (e.g. electricity); cyclicals (e.g. water transportation) and; rate sensitives (e.g. banks).

the vast majority of U.S. based water transportation companies still remain privately owned. The primary reason, given by both investor groups and investment bankers for this, is the industry's perceived high level of risk.

This risk stems from the fact that on one hand the water transportation industry is a predominantly capital intensive industry which requires huge investment outlays, while on the other hand it is subject to cyclicality which more often than not is beyond the industry's control. This cyclicality is a result of the industry serving the world economy through the transportation of world trade. It is a fact of life that the world economy goes through cycles and along with it world trade goes through cycles as well. Consequently, the water transportation industry is also subject to cycles whose amplitudes are a function of those of the world economy and the demand and supply situation in the water transportation market.

Given the above risk profile of the water transportation industry, it is the prime motive of this book to examine, and compare, this industry's risk perception over time and across industries of similar and different risk profiles. Having said that, it is worth making one last point, which is that the number of companies publicly listed for all transportation industries are relatively small in comparison to other industries, and this fact somewhat puts limitations on to the analysis.

1.7 Conclusion

The aim of this chapter has been to motivate the need for this study and places it within a finance and water transportation point of view in the literature. Following a short description of how equity asset pricing stands in the general finance theory, the chapter considers the investment decisions facing investors and the scope for industry analysis as part of the investors' decision process. The SIC system used for classification of companies into industries in this book is presented and relevant industries for analysis are identified. A background to all the industries used for comparative equity analysis of their equities in the US stock exchanges is also provided, and the rationale for selecting these particular industries is put forward.

Appendix 1: Exact SIC Definitions for the US Industries covered in the Book

SIC Major Group 44 - Water Transportation

Major Group Structure:

This major group includes establishments engaged in:

- Deep Sea Foreign Transportation Of Freight,
- Deep Sea Domestic Transportation Of Freight,
- Freight Transportation On The Great Lakes,
- Water Transportation Of Passengers,
- Water Transportation of Ferries,
- Services Incidental to Water Transportation such as Marine Cargo Handling and Towing And Tugboat Services.

SIC Major Group 45 - Air Transportation

Major Group Structure:

This major group includes establishments engaged in:

- Scheduled And Air Courier Air Transportation,
- Non-scheduled Air Transportation,
- Airports, Flying Fields and Airport Terminals.

SIC Major Group 40 - Railroad Transportation

Major Group Structure:

This major group includes establishments furnishing transportation by line-haul railroad, and switching and terminal establishments.

SIC Major Group 42 - Motor Freight Transportation And Warehousing

Major Group Structure:

This major group includes establishments furnishing:

- Local Trucking Without Storage,
- Local Trucking With Storage,
- Courier Services(Except By Air),
- Farm Product Warehousing And Storage,

- Refrigerated Warehousing And Storage,
- General Warehousing And Storage,
- Special Warehousing And Storage and
- Terminal And Joint Terminal Maintenance Facilities For Motor Freight.

SIC Major Group 4911 - Electricity

Major Group Structure:

This major group includes establishments engaged in:

- Generation, Transmission, and/or Distribution of Electric Energy for sale.

SIC Major Group 4922 - 4925 - Gas Production And Distribution

Major Group Structure:

4922 Natural Gas Transmission

Establishments engaged in Natural gas storage, Natural gas transmission, and Pipelines.

4923 Natural Gas Transmission and Distribution

Establishments engaged in Natural gas transmission and distribution

4924 Natural Gas Distribution

Establishments engaged in Natural gas distribution

4925 Mixed, Manufactured, or Liquefied Petroleum Gas Production

Establishments engaged in the manufacture and/or distribution of gas for sale, including mixtures of manufactured with natural gas such as Blue gas, Coke oven gas, Liquefied petroleum (LP) gas, Synthetic natural gas from naphtha.

SIC Major Group 29 - Petroleum Refining And Related Industries

Major Group Structure:

This major group includes establishments primarily engaged in:

- Petroleum Refining,
- Asphalt Paving And Roofing Materials,
- Miscellaneous Products Of Petroleum And Coal Lubricating Oils And Greases and Products Of Petroleum And Coal.

SIC Major Group 65 - Real Estate

Major Group Structure:

This major group includes:

- Real Estate Operators (except Developers) And Operators Of Non-residential Buildings,
- Operators Or Apartment Buildings,
- Operators Of Dwellings Other Than Apartment Buildings,
- Operators Of Residential Mobile Home Sites,
- Lessors Of Railroad Property,
- Lessors Of Real Property,
- Real Estate Agents And Managers,
- Title Abstract Offices and
- Land Subdividers And Developers.

Appendix 2: Companies used in this Book grouped according to SIC

Water Transportation Industry; SIC code: 44	Air Transportation Industry; SIC code: 45	Rail Industry; SIC code: 40	Trucks Industry; SIC code: 42
1. Alex & Baldwin	1. Airborne Freight	1. Anixter	1. Adams Resources & Energy
2. Amerada Hess	2. Alaska Air	2. Burlington Northern	2. Arnold Indus
3. American President	3. America West Airlines	3. Florida East Coast	3. Arts - Way
4. CSX	4. AMR Corp.	4. Hudson Genl	4. Chemical Leaman
5. Eastern Enterprises	5. Atlantic Southeast Airlines	5. Kansas City Southern	5. Consolidated Freightways
6. Gatx	6. Comair Hdg	6. Santa Fe Pacific	6. Coors Adolph
7. Hawaiian	7. Delta Air	7. Seaboard Corp	7. Envisource
8. International Shipholding Group	8. Kimberly - Clark	8. Westmoreland	8. Federal Express
9. Loew's Corp.	9. Mesaba Hdg		9. Frozen Food Express
10. Nicor	10. Ronson		10. Hunt J B Transport
11. Offshore Logistics	11. Rowan Cos		11. Knight Ridder
12. OMI	12. Southwest Airlines		12. Nabors
13. OSG	13. US Air Group		13. Norfolk Southern
14. Tidewater			14. Pittway
			15. Roadway
			16. Ryder System
			17. Salem Nat
			18. Savannah Foods & ind
			19. Union Pacific
			20. Unit Corp
			21. United Foods
			22. Western Waste Indus

Electricity Industry;	SIC code: 4911	Gas Industry;	SIC code: 4922-4925
1. American Elec. Power	26. Montana Power	1. Atlanta Gas	26. Questmark
2. Bangor Hydro - Elec	27. Neco Enterprises	2. Atmos Energy	27. Scana
3. Boston Edison	28. Newport	3. Bay State	28. Seagull Energy
4. Carolina & Light	29. Niagara Mohawk	4. Berkshire Brooklyn	29. Southeastern Gas
5. Central & South West Corp.	30. Northern States Power	5. Cabot	30. Southwest Gas
6. Consumer Power	31. Ohio Power	6. Cascade Nat. Gas	31. Tejas
7. Detroit Edison	32. Pacificorp	7. Chesapeake	32. Tenneco
8. Dominion Resources	33. Pannandle Eastern	8. Coastal	33. TGX Corp.
9. DPL	34. Peco Energy	9. Colonial Gas	34. USD Cities Gas
10. DQE	35. Pennsylvania Power & Light	10. Conn. NTRL Gas	35. Valero
11. Duke Power	36. Pinnacle West Capital	11. Cons. Nat Gas	36. Wash Gas
12. Eastern Utilities	37. Portland Genl corp	12. Delmava PWR	
13. El Paso Elec.	38. Potomac	13. Delta State Gas	
14. Empire Dist. Elec.	39. Puget Sound Power & light	14. Energen	
15. Entergy Corp	40. Rochester	15. Enron	
16. Florida Progress	41. Scecorp	16. Enserch	
17. FPL Group	42. Southern Co.	17. Equitable Shares	
18. Green Mountain Power	43. Texas Utilities	18. Essex County	
19. Houston	44. Tnp Enterprises	19. Harken Energy	
20. Idaho	45. Toledo Edison	20. Indiana	
21. Ipalco Enterprises	46. UGI Corp.	21. Nat Ful	
22. Long Island	47. Union Elec.	22. Northwest NTRL	
23. Magma Power	48. Upper Peninsula	23. Oneok	
24. MDU Resources	49. York Research Corp.	24. Orange	
25. Minnesota Power & light		25. Primark	

Petroleum Refinery Industry; SIC code: 29	Real Estate Industry; SIC code: 65
1. Amoco	1. Aon Corp.
2. Arabian	2. Commonwealth
3. Ashland	3. Gen. Magnaplate
4. Atlantic	4. Leisure Tech
5. Ethyl	5. New Mexico
6. Holly	6. Penn
7. Hondo	7. Providence
8. Howell	8. Tsi Inc
9. Murphy	
10. Pennzoil	
11. Petrolit	
12. Salomon	
13. Tesoro	
14. Tosco	
15. Unocal	
16. Witco	

CHAPTER 2: STATISTICAL METHODOLOGY

2.1. Introduction

The type of research methodologies used in analysing stock returns in the book is outlined in this technical chapter. The chapter begins with definitions of useful summary statistics, such as the mean, standard deviation, coefficient of variation, and their interpretation. Tests statistics for inferences on population means, proportions and differences of means, among others, are also presented.

A summary of single equation regression techniques and the way these are applied through estimation and inference are outlined, focusing on the interpretation of standard output and diagnostic tests. The single equation methodology is then extended to multiple equation systems; the methods of Multivariate Least Square (MLSQ) Regressions as well as those of Seemingly Unrelated Regression Equations (SURE) are considered. Time series, ARIMA, models form also part of the discussion. This is a chapter, which is aimed at readers who are interested in understanding the technical background used in deriving results later in the book.

2.2. Summary Statistics for a set of Data

A set of numbers which are generated by agents' actions in the market, and which can take different values if the agents were to repeat their actions, are known as random variables. For example, prices of shares in the stock exchange are determined at each point in time from the collective actions of agents operating in the market through their demand and supply decisions. The price of a share is thus a random variable, and so is the return of the share.

Investments in shares are made in the hope of making a profit, by selling the share at a higher price later on and by receiving income during the holding period in the form of dividend payments. Thus, the total return on a security (in percentage terms), j, purchased at time period t-1, at price P_{jt-1}, held for one period (perhaps a month) and sold at P_{jt}, while receiving a dividend payment of d_{jt} at the end of the holding period, is defined as[1]

$$R_{jt} = \left(\frac{P_{jt} - P_{jt-1}}{P_{jt-1}} + \frac{d_{jt}}{P_{jt-1}}\right) \times 100 \qquad (2.1)$$

Alternatively, logarithmic returns may be calculated as

$$R_{jt} = \ln\left(\frac{P_{jt} + d_{jt}}{P_{jt-1}}\right) \times 100 \qquad (2.2)$$

Given a set of time series data on the returns of a share, the average return over the period may be calculated by summing up all returns and dividing by the total number of observations. That is,

$$\overline{R}_j = \frac{\sum_{t=1}^{T} R_{jt}}{T} \qquad (2.3)$$

The popularity of the mean as a measure of average of a set of data, such as company returns, is based on a number of desirable properties it exhibits. More specifically,

(1) it is familiar to most people due to its simplicity,

(2) it can be calculated for any set of data,

(3) it is unique; a set of data can only have one mean,

(4) its statistical properties are well known, so that inferences, such as confidence intervals and hypothesis testing, are easy to make.

Other measures of average of a set of data, such as the median and the mode, exist. The former is defined as the middle value of the ordered list of observations, while the latter is defined as the most frequently occurring value in the list.

Often we are interested, not only on what is a typical – average – value of a set of company returns, but also on the variation of these returns around their average value.

---

[1] Logarithmic returns take into account continuous compounding in the reinvestment of proceeds from holding the share.

This is because the higher the variation in returns the higher is the risk undertaken by investing in that security thought to be, and visa versa for a lower variation in returns. If one considers time series data for returns, then the average of the square deviations of these returns from their mean value can provide a single figure of (average) risk involved in holding the security over the period. This measure is the variance and its square root (expressed in the unit of measurement of the original variable), the standard deviation, is defined mathematically as:

$$SD_j = \sqrt{\frac{\sum_{t=1}^{T}(R_{jt} - \overline{R_j})^2}{T-1}} \quad (2.4)$$

Considering the mathematics of equation it (2.4) may be observed that if the observations of a set of data are concentrated near the mean then the standard deviation will be small, whereas, if the opposite is true, the standard deviation will be large. In fact, according to Chebyshev's Theorem, for any kind of data at least 75% of the data must fall within 2 standard deviations of the mean.

Other measures of dispersion exist, such as the range (the difference between the highest and the lowest values of the list of observations) and the average deviation (which considers absolute rather than squared deviations of data from their mean value). However, the statistical properties of the variance and standard deviation are well known and are, as a result, the most commonly used measures of dispersion of data around their mean value.

The standard deviation and other measures of dispersion mentioned are absolute numbers. When comparisons of variation between different sets of data are of interest, a relative measure of dispersion is useful. The coefficient of variation, CV_j, by dividing the standard deviation of the data by their own mean value, provides such a relative measure in percentage terms. Mathematically,

$$CV_j = \frac{SD_j}{\overline{R}_j} x100 \quad (2.5)$$

Therefore, the higher (lower) the CV_j, the more (less) variability there is in the set of observations.

The mean, as a measure of average, and the variance, as a measure of dispersion, of a set of stock returns are also known as the first and second moments of the data. More information on the properties of the data can be conveyed through their third and fourth moments. Summary statistics that describe these are known, respectively, as the coefficients of skewness and of kurtosis. They are useful in determining more precisely the shape of the probability distribution of returns, and are standard output of statistical packages.

There are situations when two variables are related between them. For example the return of a company, R_j, may be affected by the return of the market, R_M. Statistically, one way of measuring the (linear) relationship between such variables is the covariance, defined as follows

$$C(R_j, R_M) = \frac{\sum_{t=1}^{T} (R_{jt} - \overline{R}_j)(R_{Mt} - \overline{R}_M)}{T-1} \quad (2.6)$$

It takes values between minus infinity and plus infinity. When $C(R_j,R_M)=0$ there is no relationship between the variables, when $C(R_j,R_M)>0$ there is a positive relationship between the variables (which move in the same direction), and when $C(R_j,R_M)<0$ the relationship between the variables is negative (moving in opposite directions).

The covariance suffers from a unit of measurement problem. A way to avoid this is to standardise it by dividing its value by the product of the standard deviations of the two variables. This is the correlation coefficient between the two variables and measures both the type and the strength of the relationship.

$$\rho(R_j, R_M) = \frac{C(R_j, R_M)}{SD(R_j)SD(R_M)} \quad (2.7)$$

It takes values between –1 and +1. When $\rho(R_j,R_M)=0$ there is no relationship between the variables. Values of the coefficient close to 0 indicate a weak relationship between the variables. When $\rho(R_j,R_M)>0$, there is a positive relationship between the variables (which move in the same direction), and the closer this value is to +1 the stronger is this positive relationship. When $\rho(R_j,R_M)<0$, the relationship between the variables is negative (moving in opposite directions), and the closer this value is to –1 the stronger is this negative relationship.

The autocovariance and autocorrelation coefficients are also worth defining at this point. Thus, the autocorrelation coefficient of order k, measures the correlation of values of a variable at time period t with its own lagged values at time period t-k, and is defined as follows

$$\rho_k = \frac{C(R_{jt}, R_{jt-k})}{V(R_{jt})} \tag{2.8}$$

where $C(R_{jt}, R_{jt-k})$ is the kth order autocovariance of ΔR_{jt} and $V(\Delta R_{jt})$ is the variance of ΔR_{jt}. r_k may be used to denote the sample autocorrelation coefficients, which are the sample equivalents of these.

2.3. Inference (Hypothesis Testing or Confidence Intervals)

All the above summary statistics are random variables, as their value would change for different samples of data. Knowledge of the distribution of each statistic facilitates inferences, regarding the true value of population parameters. In this book we are concerned with inferences on the population mean, the population proportion, the coefficients of skewness and of kurtosis and on differences between the means of two sets of data. For example, it may be of interest to an investor to test whether the average return of a company is significantly different from zero.

The central limit theorem facilitates inferences on the mean. It states that, if sampling is carried from a set of data with mean μ and variance σ^2 (with unknown distribution), as the sample size increases the sampling distribution of the sample mean will tend to follow a normal distribution with mean equal to the population mean, μ, and variance which is equal to the population variance, σ^2, divided by the number of observations, say T, in the sample; the distribution of the sample mean is normal, regardless of the distribution of the original data. When the population variance is not known, and the sample variance is used instead in the calculation (derived from equation (2.4)), the distribution of the sample mean follows a student-t distribution with T-1 degrees of freedom. Thus, the following statistic is relevant for hypothesis testing in relation to the mean of returns of a security, μ, say.

$$t - stat = \frac{\bar{R} - \mu}{SD / \sqrt{T}} \sim t(T-1) \tag{2.9}$$

where $SD/\sqrt{T}$ is the estimated standard error (SE) of the sample mean return, $\bar{R}$. Once an estimate of the t-stat from equation (2.9) becomes available this value is compared with critical values from a t-distribution (available in statistical tables), at the appropriate level of significance (usually 1%, 5% or 10%), and a decision is taken on whether to reject or not reject the null hypothesis.

Similarly, to test hypotheses about the true value of the population proportion, Π, given a value for the sample proportion, obtained from a sample of size T, the following statistic is appropriate:

$$Z = \frac{p - \Pi}{\sqrt{\frac{p(1-p)}{T}}} \sim N(0,1) \tag{2.10}$$

The relevant test statistics used for inferences on the true values of the population coefficients of skewness, SK, and of kurtosis, KU, are, respectively:

$$\sqrt{\frac{T}{6}} SK \underset{as}{\sim} N(0,1) \tag{2.11}$$

$$\sqrt{\frac{T}{24}} KU \underset{as}{\sim} N(0,1) \tag{2.12}$$

The test statistic to test hypotheses for differences between two population means, μ_1-μ_2, when the standard errors, SE_1 and SE_2, of the means are estimated from sample data (with sample sizes T1 and T2) is:

$$t - stat = \frac{(\overline{R}_1 - \overline{R}_2) - (\mu_1 - \mu_2)}{\sqrt{\frac{S^2}{T1} + \frac{S^2}{T2}}} \sim t(T1 + T2 - 2) \tag{2.13}$$

where $$S^2 = \frac{(T1-1)SE_1^{\,2} + (T2-1)SE_2^{\,2}}{T1 + T2 - 2}$$

The appropriate statistic for hypothesis testing on values of the population correlation coefficient, ρ, is

$$Z = \frac{Z' - \mu_Z{}'}{\sigma_Z{}'} \sim N(0,1) \tag{2.14}$$

where Z' is given by the Fisher transformation, $Z' = \frac{1}{2}\ln(\frac{1+r}{1-r})$, and $\mu_{Z'} = \frac{1}{2}\ln(\frac{1+\rho}{1-\rho})$, $\sigma^2_{Z'} = \frac{1}{T-3}$; r and T are the sample correlation coefficient and the number of observations used for estimation of r, respectively.

Summary statistics (first, second, third and fourth moments) of a random variable – say, the return of a security - do not take into account the possibility that the variation in the return of an individual stock can be (partly) explained by the variation in the return of some other variable, such as the market return. Such conditioning of one variable on another facilitates a better prediction of returns. It requires use of regression methods to estimate such relationships. These regression techniques are examined in the next section.

2.4. Single Equation Regression Methods

Consider the case where the return on the equity of company j, R_{jt}, at any point in time is linearly related to the return on the market, R_{Mt} (the market portfolio of stocks, the S&P500, say for the USA). The following stochastic equation captures this

$$R_{jt} = \alpha_j + \beta_j R_{Mt} + \varepsilon_{jt} \tag{2.15}$$

where ε_{jt} is a normally distributed stochastic error term, capturing all other factors affecting the company return apart from the market return, but which have too small an effect on the company return to be included explicitly in the systematic part of the model. Thus, the error term (also known as a white noise error term) is independent and identically distributed with a mean of 0 and a constant variance, the latter being equal to the conditional variance of the company return, R_{jt}. In addition, it is assumed that both company and market returns are stationary variables, in the sense that a shock to either variable will be eradicated quickly and have no long run effect on its distribution. The assumption is realistic as returns are formed as percentage changes of prices (prices are non-stationary, I(1), variables), and yields (which are stationary, I(0), variables)[2].

Alternatively, in estimating these types of equations in finance (which is the approach we follow in this book), the excess return of the company stock is used as the dependent variable and the excess market return is used as the independent variable in the regression equation.[3] The following equation shows that.

$$XR_{jt} = \alpha_j + \beta_j XR_{Mt} + \varepsilon_{jt} \tag{2.16}$$

The above equation then splits the variation in the company return into a systematic part, measured by $\alpha_j + \beta_j XR_{Mt}$ and a non-systematic part measured by ε_{jt}. β_j and α_j are the parameters of the model. The former measures the sensitivity of the stock excess return to changes in the expected excess return on the market portfolio, while the latter indicates deviations from equilibrium pricing; if α_j is positive it implies that the stock is

---

[2] The stationarity of a variable, say the stock return, may be tested through the Augmented Dickey Fuller (ADF) test, see Dickey and Fuller (1979, 1981) and Harris (1995). An example of the equation underlying this test is $\Delta R_{jt} = \mu + \gamma \text{ Trend} + \delta R_{jt-1} + \sum_{i=1}^{p} \psi_i \Delta R_{jt-i} + \varepsilon_{jt}$, where the null hypothesis of a unit root, H_0: $\delta = 0$, versus a left-sided alternative of H_1:$\delta < 0$, is tested using critical values tabulated by MacKinnon(1991). Prior to performing ADF tests the lag-length, p, is selected using Akaike (1973) or Schwarz (1978) information criteria, see Harris (1995). These are defined as AIC=*-2(LL–K)*, SBIC=*-2(LL–0.5KlogT), respectively,* where *LL* is the maximum value of the log-likelihood function of the ADF regression, *K* is the number of regressors and *T* is the number of observations. These criteria are introduced in order to account for the property of parsimony in estimated models. Thus, models with smaller values of these criteria are preferable to those with larger ones.

[3] The excess return of a stock (the market, XR_{Mt}), XR_{jt}, is defined as the return of the stock (the market) minus the risk free rate; that is, $XR_{jt} = R_{jt} - R_{ft}$, ($XR_{Mt} = R_{Mt} - R_{ft}$), where R_{ft} is the risk free rate - for the USA, the one month treasury bill rate.

underpriced and if it is negative that the stock is overpriced. Regarding β_j, assets with β_j greater (lower) than unity carry above (below) "average" systematic risk, and investors would therefore require higher (lower) expected return to hold it.

The above, single index model, has been extended in the finance literature to include other factors that may influence company returns. These may be company specific or macroeconomic factors. For simplicity, we extend equation (2.16) to include the earnings price ratio, E/P, and unanticipated changes in oil prices, UOG, as such representative variables of each set.

$$XR_{it} = \beta_{0i} + \beta_{1i}\, XR_{Mt} + \beta_{2i}\, (E/P)_{it} + \beta_{3i}\, UOG_t + \varepsilon_{it} \qquad (2.17)$$

A compact way of writing equations (2.16) or (2.17) in matrix form is.

$$\underline{y} = X\,\underline{\beta} + \underline{\varepsilon} \quad ; \quad \underline{\varepsilon} \sim (\underline{0}, \sigma^2 I_T) \qquad (2.18)$$

or, given a sample of observations for the dependent variable, $\underline{y}$, and the independent variables, X, the sample regression model becomes:

$$\underline{y} = X\,\underline{b} + \underline{e} \qquad (2.19)$$

where $\underline{y}$ is a (T x 1) vector of time series observations on the dependent variable, $\underline{y}$, X is a (T x k) matrix of explanatory variables with 1's as elements in the first column and each of the other columns representing time series observations on each of the explanatory variables. $\underline{e}$ is a (T x 1) vector of residuals (the sample equivalent of the error terms, $\underline{\varepsilon}$ in equation (2.18)), and $\underline{b}$ is a (kx1) vector of coefficients, $\underline{b}=(b_1,\ldots,b_k)'$ (the sample equivalent of the population parameters, $\underline{\beta}=(\beta_1,\ldots,\beta_k)'$ in equation (2.18)).

2.4.1. The problem of Estimation

Given the set of time series data for each of the variables entering the regression model in equations (2.16), (2.17) or (2.18)/(2.19), the problem of estimation is to choose the parameter values $\underline{b}$, say in (2.19), that will minimise the sum of square deviations of the actual from the fitted values. Equivalently, the objective function should be that the sum of squared residuals is minimised. Mathematically

$$\text{Minimise } S = \underline{e}'\,\underline{e} = (\underline{y} - X\,\underline{b})'\,(\underline{y} - X\,\underline{b}) \qquad (2.20)$$

Where $\underline{b}$ are the sample equivalents of the population parameters $\underline{\beta}$, and $\underline{e}$ are the residuals, the sample equivalents of the error terms $\underline{\varepsilon}$.

It can be shown (see for example Pindyck and Rubinfeld, 1991) that the Ordinary Least Squares (OLS) parameters, obtained by solving the above minimisation problem, are:

$$\underline{b} = (X'X)^{-1}\,X'\,\underline{y} \qquad (2.21)$$

The above OLS estimators, $\underline{b}$ of $\underline{\beta}$, are the Best Linear Unbiased Estimators (BLUE)[4]. They are unbiased (on average they are equal to the true parameters) and are best in the sense that no other estimator has smaller variance.

An alternative way of estimating the parameters of interest in (2.19) is through the maximisation of the following log-likelihood function.

$$LL = -(T/2)\ln 2\pi - (T/2)\ln\sigma^2 - (1/2\sigma^2)\,(y-X\underline{b})'(y-X\underline{b}) \qquad (2.22)$$

Maximizing LL with respect to $\underline{b}$ is equivalent to the minimisation problem in (2.20). As a result, the Maximum Likelihood (ML) estimators, $\underline{\tilde{b}}$, are equivalent to the OLS estimators in (2.20). In addition, the maximisation problem of LL gives the following

ML estimator of σ^2, $\tilde{\sigma}^2 = \underline{\tilde{e}}'\underline{\tilde{e}}/T$. This is a biased estimator of σ^2, but it is asymptotically unbiased.

2.4.2. The problem of Inference

For inference, the assumption of normality of the error terms and an estimate of the variance, V(b), of the estimator b is needed. The latter can be shown to be

$$\hat{V}(\underline{b}) = \hat{\sigma}^2 (X'X)^{-1} \tag{2.23}$$

where an unbiased estimate of σ^2 is given by $\hat{\sigma}^2 = \underline{e}'\underline{e} / (T-k)$. The latter is equivalent to the conditional variance of the residuals, the square root of which is known as the standard error of regression.

Thus, given the assumption of normality and equations (2.20) and (2.23), a short hand notation of writing the distribution of b is:

$$\underline{b} \sim N\left((X'X)^{-1} X' \underline{y},\ \sigma^2 (X'X)^{-1} \right) \tag{2.24}$$

The following t statistic can be used for inferences on the population parameters

$$t-stat = \frac{\underline{b} - \underline{\beta}}{\hat{SE}(\underline{b})} \sim t(T-k) \tag{2.25}$$

where $\hat{SE}(\underline{b})$ is the estimated standard error of b, estimated as the square root of the estimate in equation (2.23), and k are the number of estimated parameters in the regression model.

---

[4] This is also known as the Gauss-Markov Theorem.

2.4.3. Goodness of Fit and some Diagnostic Tests

Goodness of fit in multivariate regression models is usually measured by the coefficient of multiple determination, R^2, or the adjusted coefficient of multiple determination, else known as adjusted R^2 or R-bar squared, $\overline{R}^2$. They both measure the percentage of variation in y explained by X. Mathematically they are defined as

$$R^2 = 1 - \frac{\Sigma e_t^2}{\Sigma (Y_t - \bar{Y})^2} \tag{2.26}$$

and

$$\overline{R}^2 = 1 - \frac{Var(e_t)}{Var(Y_t)} = 1 - \frac{\Sigma e_t^2 / (T-k)}{\Sigma (Y_t - \bar{Y})^2 / (T-1)} \tag{2.27}$$

The closer the value of either statistic is to 1 the better the fit of the model, and visa-versa for values close to 0. The R-bar square is preferred in regression models with more than one explanatory variable, as of insignificant variables are included in the model its value does not increase. This is in contrast to the value of R^2, which always increases if another variable is added as an explanatory variable in the model no matter whether it is significant or not.

The standard error of regression, $\hat{\sigma}$, is also a relative measure of goodness of fit of regression models. Models with lower $\hat{\sigma}$'s are preferable.

The Durbin-Watson (DW) statistic is useful in detecting whether the residuals are identically and independently distributed (no autocorrelation assumption). It is defined as:

$$DW = \frac{\sum_{t=2}^{T} (e_t - e_{t-1})^2}{\sum_{t=2}^{T} e_t^2} \tag{2.28}$$

When DW = 4 there is perfect negative correlation, when DW = 2 there is no auto-correlation, while for DW = 0 there is perfect positive correlation. To identify whether the null of no autocorrelation is valid, the observed values of the DW statistic are compared to critical values obtained in standard econometrics books, such as Pindyck and Rubinfeld (1991). The statistic is not valid when lagged variables of the dependent variable are included in the equation. This is not an issue in this book, but alternative tests exist, such as Durbin's alternative h statistic, which rectify the problem.

Often it is important to test whether the estimated coefficients of the regression model, such as those of equation (2.15), are stable over time. Chow's stability test may be used to this effect. It amounts to running the regression equation for the two subperiods, and testing first the equality of variance in the two subperiods through the following F-test.

$$F = \frac{S_1^2}{S_2^2} \sim F(T_1 - k,\ T_2 - k) \qquad (2.29)$$

If accepted, then the regression model is estimated over the whole period and for each sub-period, saving the RSS (Residual Sum of Squares) from each equation i.e. RSS_T, RSS_1, RSS_2, respectively. The following F-statistic is Chow's test-statistic for testing the stability of the coefficients over the two subperiods:

$$F = \frac{[RSS_T - (RSS_1 + RSS_2)]/k}{(RSS_1 + RSS_2)\ /\ (T_1 + T_2 - 2k)} \sim F(k,\ T_1 + T_2 - 2k) \qquad (2.30)$$

Critical values for the F distribution are tabulated in standard statistical tables.

Alternatively, one could run the following dummy variable sample regression equation, for the single index model, say, with the binary variable, d_t, included. The latter takes the value of unity in the second period and zero otherwise.

$$XR_{jt} = \alpha_{1j} + \alpha_{2j}\, d_t + \beta_{1j}\, XR_{Mt} + \beta_{2j}\, (d_t\, XR_{Mt}) + e_{jt} \qquad (2.31)$$

The coefficients of the binary variables α_{2j} and β_{2j}, measure the differential effects of the second period over the first period for the constant and the excess market return, respectively. t-statistics on the individual coefficients indicate such significance.

If β_{1j} and β_{2j} are jointly significantly different from 0 then a separate regression (where both constant and slope are different) is appropriate for each period. The following F-statistic may be used to test this.

$$F = \frac{(RRSS - URSS\ /\ r)}{URSS/\ (T-k)} \sim F(r, T-k) \tag{2.32}$$

where, RRSS and URSS are the Restricted and Unrestricted Residual Sum of Squares; the former come from the model without the dummy variables, while the latter comes from the more general model with the dummy variables included in. r is the number of restrictions in moving from the unrestricted to the restricted model; in this case r=2, as the dummy variable coefficients are jointly set to 0. Finally, T-k are the degrees of freedom of the unrestricted model.

The above test may be expressed in terms of R^2's as:

$$F = \frac{(R_u^2 - R_R^2)/\ r}{(1 - R_u^2)\ /T-k} \sim F(r, T-k) \tag{2.33}$$

where R_u^2 is the R^2 of the unrestricted model, and R_R^2 is the R^2 of the restricted model.

The idea above can be generalised to tests of whether estimated relationships differ under alternative conditions; for example, under bullish and bearish market conditions, as in chapter 4 of this book.

2.4.4. The significance of the regression model assumptions and GLS estimation

We have assumed that the covariance matrix of the vector $\underline{y}$, and therefore of the vector $\underline{\varepsilon}$, in equation (2.17), is $E[\underline{\varepsilon}\ \underline{\varepsilon}'] = \sigma^2 I_T$. This assumption, that the elements of the random vector $\underline{\varepsilon}$ are independent and identically distributed (that is, that they are uncorrelated and have identical variance), may be changed to involve more general structures. For instance, that $E[\underline{\varepsilon}\ \underline{\varepsilon}'] = \sigma^2\ \Omega$, where Ω is a known real positive definite symmetric matrix. Depending on the precise form of Ω, the error term may be heteroskedastic (variable variance, σ^2, between observations), autocorrelated (the elements of the error term are correlated are correlated between themselves), a combination of both, or perhaps follow complicated VAR (Vector Auto-Regressive) processes.

Thus, assuming that the model now is

$$\underline{y} = X\,\underline{\beta} + \underline{\varepsilon} \quad ; \quad \underline{\varepsilon} \sim (\underline{0}, \sigma^2\,\Omega) \tag{2.34}$$

OLS or ML estimation yields estimators which are unbiased but inefficient. It can be shown (see Judge et al, 1988, appendix A, section A11), that since Ω is a positive definite matrix, a matrix P with the property $P\Omega P' = I_T$ always exists. This matrix can be used to transform the model in (2.34) to:

$$P\,\underline{y} = P\,X\,\underline{\beta} + P\,\underline{\varepsilon} \qquad \text{or} \qquad \underline{y}^* = X^*\,\underline{\beta} + \underline{\varepsilon}^* \tag{2.35}$$

where $\underline{y}^*=P\underline{y}$, $X^*=PX$ and $\underline{\varepsilon}^*=P\underline{\varepsilon}$. The transformed error vector has a distribution $\underline{\varepsilon}^*\sim(\underline{0}, \sigma^2\ I_T)$, since $E[\underline{\varepsilon}^*\underline{\varepsilon}^{*\prime}]=\sigma^2 E[P\underline{\varepsilon}\ \underline{\varepsilon}'P']= \sigma^2 P\Omega P'=\sigma^2 I_T$. OLS may now be applied to the transformed model. This estimator of $\underline{\beta}$ is the GLS (Generalized Least Squares) or Aitken estimator, which has a distribution:

$$\underline{b}^* \sim ((X^{*\prime}\ X^*)^{-1}\ X^{*\prime}\ \underline{y},\ \sigma^2\ (X^{*\prime}\ X^*)^{-1}) \tag{2.36}$$

or, in terms of the original data,

$$\underline{b} \sim ((X'\Omega^{-1}X)^{-1}\ X'\Omega^{-1}\ \underline{y},\ \sigma^2\ (X'\Omega^{-1}X)^{-1}) \tag{2.37}$$

That is: $\underline{b} = (X'\Omega^{-1}X)^{-1} X'\Omega^{-1} \underline{y}$ and $V(\underline{b}) = \sigma^2 (X'\Omega^{-1}X)^{-1}$.

The GLS estimator is BLUE, and if normality of $\underline{\varepsilon}$ holds, the distribution of $\underline{b}$ is normal. In addition, the ML estimator is equivalent to it.

2.5. Multiple Equation Regression Methods

As the primary interest in this book is in estimating industry α's and β's, say in a model like (2.16) or (2.17), there are two ways of estimating these average (over companies) – industry - values. One is by running a time series regression for each company, within the same industry, and then calculating the average over α's or β's to get the industry average. The other way is by estimating a system of equations for each industry, and imposing the restriction of a common α or β across equations. The econometrics of this second method are examined in this section.

This second method has the computational advantage of estimating the industry averages in one step through Multivariate Least Square Methods (MLSQ). In addition, the option of taking into account the possible cross equation correlation, which may be prevalent in company returns within the same sector, can be taken in a variation of MLSQ known as Seemingly Unrelated Regression Equations (SURE).[5] This adjustment in the cross-sectional correlation in the residual returns across companies, within the same industry, leads to more efficient estimates than those obtained by using OLS on each individual company, see Judge et al (1985) and Zellner(1962).

Consider the following system of n equations, one equation like (2.18) for each equity stock. If (2.18) represents(2.16) or (2.17) with common coefficients appearing across equations, the system must be `pooled' together for estimation. Assuming a sample of T observations for each of the n equities, then we can write the system in stacked form as follows:

[5] This is equivalent to using GLS in a multi-equation setting, Zellner(1962).

$$\begin{pmatrix} \underline{y}_1 \\ \underline{y}_2 \\ \cdot \\ \cdot \\ \cdot \\ \underline{y}_n \end{pmatrix} = \begin{bmatrix} X_1 & 0 & . & . & . & 0 \\ 0 & X_2 & . & . & . & 0 \\ . & . & . & . & . & . \\ . & . & . & . & . & . \\ . & . & . & . & . & . \\ 0 & 0 & . & . & . & X_n \end{bmatrix} \begin{pmatrix} \underline{\beta}_1 \\ \underline{\beta}_2 \\ \cdot \\ \cdot \\ \cdot \\ \underline{\beta}_n \end{pmatrix} + \begin{pmatrix} \underline{\varepsilon}_1 \\ \underline{\varepsilon}_2 \\ \cdot \\ \cdot \\ \cdot \\ \underline{\varepsilon}_n \end{pmatrix} \tag{2.38}$$

where $\underline{y}_i$ and $\underline{\varepsilon}_i$ are (Tx1) vectors, $\underline{\beta}_i$ are (kx1) parameter vectors and X_i are (Txk) matrices, for each of the i=1,...,n equations in the system. Each equation explains the variation of the dependent variable $\underline{y}_i$, i=1,...,n, over time.

where $\underline{y}_i$ and $\underline{\varepsilon}_i$ are (Tx1) vectors, $\underline{\beta}_i$ are (kx1) parameter vectors and X_i are (Txk) matrices, for each of the i=1,...,n equations in the system. Each equation explains the variation of the dependent variable $\underline{y}_i$, i=1,...,n, over time.

Assume, for simplicity, that for each equation, $\underline{\varepsilon}_i \sim (\underline{0}, \sigma_i^2 I_T)$. That is, the 'classical' assumptions of the single equation model are true. The above system in matrix form becomes:

$$Y = X B + E, \qquad \text{with} \qquad E \sim (0, \Sigma \otimes I_T) \tag{2.39}$$

where $\otimes$ denotes the Kronecker product in matrix operations. Y and E are (nT x 1) vectors of dependent variables and error terms, respectively, X is the (nT x nk) matrix of explanatory variables and B is the (nk x 1) vector of coefficients. Also, Σ is the variance-covariance matrix of the residuals between equations. It takes the form $\Sigma=[\sigma_{ij}]=E[\underline{\varepsilon}_i\underline{\varepsilon}_j']$, $\forall$ i,j=1,...,n, where $[\sigma_{ij}]$ denotes the (n x n) matrix with elements ranked by i,j. More specifically

$$\Sigma = \begin{bmatrix} E(\underline{\varepsilon}_1\, \underline{\varepsilon}_1') & E(\underline{\varepsilon}_1\, \underline{\varepsilon}_2') & \dots & E(\underline{\varepsilon}_1\, \underline{\varepsilon}_n') \\ E(\underline{\varepsilon}_2\, \underline{\varepsilon}_1') & E(\underline{\varepsilon}_2\, \underline{\varepsilon}_2') & \dots & E(\underline{\varepsilon}_2\, \underline{\varepsilon}_n') \\ \vdots & \vdots & \dots & \vdots \\ E(\underline{\varepsilon}_n\, \underline{\varepsilon}_1') & E(\underline{\varepsilon}_n\, \underline{\varepsilon}_2') & \dots & E(\underline{\varepsilon}_n\, \underline{\varepsilon}_n') \end{bmatrix} = \begin{bmatrix} \sigma_{11} & \sigma_{12} & \dots & \sigma_{1n} \\ \sigma_{21} & \sigma_{22} & \dots & \sigma_{2n} \\ \vdots & \vdots & \dots & \vdots \\ \sigma_{n1} & \sigma_{n2} & \dots & \sigma_{nn} \end{bmatrix} \tag{2.40}$$

If there is no relationship between the individual equations (i.e. if there are no cross-equation correlations in the errors $\Sigma=[\sigma_{ij}]=0, \forall$ i,j in (2.40)), the error term in (2.39) becomes $E\sim(0, \sigma_{ij}^2 \otimes I_T)$. The OLS estimators may be obtained from the 'pooled' system (2.39) by minimizing the objective function $S(B)=(Y-XB)'(Y-XB)$. The estimators are: $B=(X'X)^{-1}X'Y$, which are BLUE. These are equivalent to applying OLS separately to each individual equation, and are the same as the ML estimators, for the same reasons as with the single equation case. If estimated as a system, say through ML methods, (2.39) will give the MLSQ estimators.

2.5.1. Seemingly Unrelated Regression Equations (SURE)

Often, even though the equations may seem unrelated, if they are used to model a set of related economic functions (e.g. our set of single or multiple index equations within the same industry), there might be some relationship between the equations emanating from some common unmeasurable variable included in the error terms. In such cases, the error terms are correlated across individual equations.

Just as with the single equation case (when the covariance matrix of the vector (is not of the fixed scalar identity type), OLS estimators in a SURE model are unbiased and consistent, but their efficiency can be improved by using the information contained in the contemporaneously correlated errors, and in the possible inter-relationships between the explanatory variables across equations. This contemporaneous correlation is reflected in the error term $E\sim(0, \Omega)$, where $\Omega=\Sigma\otimes I_T$ (with $\Sigma\neq0$ for some $i\neq j$) is some known real positive definite symmetric matrix of order (nT x nT). Then, estimating the equations jointly by GLS yields the BLUE, Zellner(1962). The SURE estimators are obtained by minimizing the objective function

$$S(B) = (Y-XB)' (\Sigma^{-1}\otimes I_T) (Y-XB) \tag{2.41}$$

They are distributed as:

$$B^* \sim ((X'\Omega^{-1}X)^{-1}X'\Omega^{-1} Y, \ (X'\Omega^{-1}X)^{-1}) \tag{2.42}$$

or in terms of the original data:

$$B^* \sim ((X' (\Sigma^{-1} \otimes I_T) X)^{-1} X' (\Sigma^{-1} \otimes I_T) Y, \quad (X' (\Sigma^{-1} \otimes I_T) X)^{-1}) \tag{2.43}$$

Assuming the residuals follow a multivariate normal distribution, then the distribution of the above GLS (SURE) estimators are also normal. In addition, the ML estimators are equivalent to the above.

2.5.2. SURE Estimation with Unknown Covariance Matrix

In most cases Σ is unknown and B^* cannot be estimated, unless an estimate of Σ is formulated. In such a case $\hat{B}^*$ may be obtained in two stages. In the first stage, run each individual equation in (2.38) by least squares and obtain the residuals $\underline{e}_i = (\underline{y}_i - X_i \underline{b}_i)$. Use these to find an estimate $\hat{\Sigma}$ of Σ, where $\hat{\Sigma} = [\hat{\sigma}_{ij}]$ for all i,j=1,...n, and $\hat{\sigma}_{ij} = \underline{e}'\underline{e}/T$ are the estimated variances and covariances of Σ in (2.40). In the second stage, use $\hat{\Sigma}$ to obtain $\hat{B}^*$ as in (2.43) with Σ replaced by $\hat{\Sigma}$. These are the SURE estimators proposed by Zellner(1962).

In the above two step procedure, $\hat{\sigma}_{ij}$ is biased in finite samples because of the T in the denominator. An unbiased estimator of σ_{ij}, when the number of explanatory variables in each equation are the same, is $\hat{\sigma}_{ij} = \underline{e}'\underline{e}/(T-k)$, $\forall$ i,j=1,...,n. When the number of explanatory variables across equations are different, one may find the average number of coefficients per equation (K/n) (where $K=\Sigma_i k_i$), and use (T-(K/n)) as a divisor to obtain an unbiased $\hat{\sigma}_{ij}$.

An alternative, iterative estimator of B may be obtained as an extension of the above SURE estimator. Thus, given the first two steps above, in the third step use $\hat{B}^*$ obtained in the second step to find a new estimate of Σ, $\hat{\hat{\Sigma}}$, through $\hat{\sigma}_{ij} = (y_i - X_i\hat{\beta}_i^*)'(y_j - X_j\hat{\beta}_j^*)/T$. In the fourth step use $\hat{\hat{\sigma}}_{ij}$ to find a new estimator for B. This procedure is continued until convergence. Under normality, the estimator obtained is consistent and asymptotically efficient, Gallant(1975). It can be shown, Magnus(1978), that when E (or equivalently Y) follows a multivariate normal distribution the latter estimator is the MLE. Under appropriate conditions both the SURE and the iterative SURE estimator have the same limiting distribution.

Asymptotically, the choice of the divisor in estimating $\hat{\sigma}_{ij}$ does not influence the properties of $\hat{B}*$; it remains an unbiased and consistent estimator of B. The small sample properties have been investigated by a number of authors, with different conclusions. Their common ground is that $\hat{B}*$ is more efficient than the OLS estimator, provided the correlation between the disturbances amongst equations is not too low, see Judge et al (1985, p. 469-470).

2.5.3. Properties of SURE Estimators

There are two conditions under which both the linear and the non-linear SURE estimators are identical to the OLS:

1. When there is no contemporaneous correlation, in which case the covariance matrix Σ is diagonal and $\Sigma=[\sigma_{ij}]=0$, all $i\neq j$.
2. When the explanatory variables across equations are identical. That is, for all equations $X_1 = \ldots = X_N = \overline{X}$ (say), so that the matrix X of (2.38)/(2.39) becomes $X=(I_n\otimes \overline{X})$. Then $(X'(\Sigma^{-1}\otimes I)X)$ of (2.43) becomes:

$$X'\,(\Sigma^{-1}\otimes I)\,X = (I\otimes \overline{X}\,')\,(\Sigma^{-1}\otimes I)\,(I\otimes \overline{X}\,) = \Sigma^{-1}\otimes(\overline{X}\,'\overline{X}\,) \tag{2.44}$$

Using this in (2.43)to find B* we get:

$$\begin{aligned} B* &= (\Sigma^{-1}\otimes(\overline{X}\,'\,\overline{X}\,))^{-1}\,(I\otimes \overline{X}\,)\,(\Sigma^{-1}\otimes I)\,Y \\ &= (\Sigma\otimes(\overline{X}\,'\,\overline{X}\,)^{-1})\,(I\otimes \overline{X}\,)\,(\Sigma^{-1}\otimes I)\,Y \\ &= (I\otimes(\overline{X}\,'\,\overline{X}\,)^{-1}\,\overline{X}\,')\,Y \end{aligned} \tag{2.45}$$

which is nothing but the OLS estimator applied to each equation separately. In either case there is no gain in efficiency by estimating the equations jointly, and it is `best' if OLS is used.

So far, we have seen that, if there is any type of relationship between the equations (such as a system with error related equations in some way), taking account of this information by estimating the equations jointly in a SURE system results in more efficient estimates. This is the case when the explanatory variables of each equation are not all the same, such as in equation (2.17) where the term E/P differs between individual companies (even though XR_M and UOG would be the same across equations), say within the water transportation sector. However, in a model where all the explanatory variables are the same across equations, such as if only macroeconomic variables are included on the right hand side of the equation, OLS on each individual equation is appropriate. If a common coefficient is imposed on each macrofactor MLSQ can be used without the assumption of cross equation correlation.

2.6. Autoregressive Integrated Moving Average Models (ARIMA) models

The regression models examined so far in this chapter are structural econometric models. That is, the variation in a variable of interest is thought to be explained better if conditioned on one or more other variables. In another set, of time series models, a variable of interest, say Y, may be explained in terms of its own history (past values) and a set of past error components. Such a variable has to be stationary before decisions are made on the appropriate lag structure of the autoregressive (AR) and moving average (MA) components that need to be included in the modelled series. For example, if Y is a non-stationary series of order one[6], as judged, say by a ADF test and its autocorrelation and partial autocorrelation functions, then the variable has to be modelled in its first difference form, ΔY_t ($=Y_t - Y_{t-1}$). The following expression indicates an ARIMA(p,1,q) model that may be used to model the series, where p denotes the number of autoregressive terms (AR), q the number of moving average terms (MA) and

[6] A variable is non-stationary of order one, I(1) if it needs to be differenced once in order to become stationary.

1 the number of times that the variable needs to be differenced to achieve stationarity (I=1 in this case).

$$\Delta Y_t = \sum_{i=1}^{p} \Delta Y_{t-i} + \sum_{j=0}^{q} \Delta \varepsilon_{t-j} \qquad (2.46)$$

The lag structure of the AR and MA components in the above model may be decided through Schwarz (SBIC) or Akaike (AIC) criteria, as defined earlier, and by ensuring that the residuals are white noise. These are tested, say for 20th order autocorrelation, through the following Box-Pierce Q-statistic.

$$Q(20) = T\sum_{k=1}^{s} r_{r_k}^2 \sim \chi^2(s) \qquad (2.47)$$

where T are the number of observations, and r_k are the sample autocorrelation coefficients of order k. Standard chi-squared tables may be used to compare the observed value of the statistic with relevant critical values. When $\chi^2_{obs} > \chi^2_{crit}$, the null hypothesis of no autocorrelation is rejected.

ARIMA models[7] are used in the book to filter out the anticipated components of macroeconomic series, such as oil prices, used as explanatory variables in multi-index models. Thus, the macroeconomic series are examined first for stationarity. If they are found non-stationary, they are differenced until they become stationary and the new variable is then modelled in an ARMA structure. The fitted values provide the anticipated part of the series, while the residuals are estimates of the unexpected component of the series.

2.7. Conclusion

This technical chapter has examined summary statistics, single and multiple equation regression models, as well as time series ARIMA models used for the purposes of this

[7] ARIMA models are related to structural regression models, and may be shown to be reduced forms of the latter.

book. It is written in such a way so as to enable the discerning reader to follow the technical parts of the analysis. It is not an econometrics handbook, but merely an aid to the empirical parts of the book, and skipping through it will not result in loss of continuity. However, it is a bonus for those interested on technical material underlying the results, and an aid for replicating similar research for researchers.

CHAPTER 3: DATA DEFINITIONS, PROPERTIES, TRANSFORMATIONS

3.1 Introduction

In earlier chapters it was suggested that the models which will be used for industry analysis are the CAPM, and multi index models which include microeconomic and macroeconomic factors that may drive returns. Data are needed for the variables entering each of the above models in order to estimate them. Some of these variables are not readily available, but have to be constructed from more basic data. These data transformations, necessary to derive the final variables which are used in the estimated models, as well as the identification of sources of these data, are described in the next section of this chapter. Section 3.3 shows summary statistics describing the properties of the data for the water transportation industry over the period analysed. The statistics are presented in such a way so as to consider whether the total risk of the water transportation industry is different from that of the "average" company in the market, and also to provide some information on the stationarity of these returns. The final section of the chapter concludes.

3.2 Models and Variables

The type of variables needed for estimation in empirical equations in subsequent chapters of the book are summarised in equation (3.1), which is a version of the model used for empirical analysis in chapter 7. It is the most general equation in the book, and encompasses models in other chapters as special cases. These are the CAPM of chapter 4 and the multi-index models of chapters 5 and 6 incorporating microeconomic and macroeconomic factors, respectively.

$$XR_{ijt}=f\{XR_{Mt}, E/P_{ijt}, ME_{ijt}, BE/ME_{ijt}, A/ME_{ijt}, A/BE_{ijt}, UMIP_{it}, UI_{it}, UTS_{it}, UOG_{it}, UCG_{it}) + \varepsilon_{ijt} \quad (3.1)$$

where j is the company in industry i, t=1984:7,...,1995:6, XR_{ijt} are company j excess returns and XR_{Mt} are market excess returns. These are defined respectively as

$$XR_{ijt} = R_{ijt} - R_{ft} \qquad \text{and} \qquad XR_{Mt} = R_{Mt} - R_{ft} \qquad (3.2)$$

Where, R_{ijt}, R_{Mt} and R_{ft} are monthly returns for company j in industry i, market returns (using the S&P500 as the proxy for the market), and the risk free rate (that is, the one-month treasury bill rate for the USA), respectively.

As explained in chapter 2, total monthly returns on shares may be defined as in equations (2.1) and (2.2). In our analysis we use logarithmic returns, which take into account continuous compounding, with the formula used repeated here for convenience.

$$R_{ijt} = \ln\left(\frac{P_{ijt} + d_{ijt}}{P_{ijt-1}}\right) \qquad (3.3)$$

where P_{ijt-1} is the price of security j in industry i, purchased at time period t-1, held for one month and sold at price P_{ijt}, while receiving a dividend payment of d_{ijt} at the end of the holding period. The same definition is used to calculate monthly market returns, using values of the S&P500, instead of security prices, in equation (3.3) to define returns.

Data for these original variables on prices and dividends for each listed company in every industry[1] are collected from DataStream International Service. Thus, for the water transportation industry data are collected for each of the 28 companies which are continually listed over the whole sample period. This sample of 28 companies represents all US listed water transportation companies for the whole ten-year period 1985 – 1994.[2]

---

[1] These are the industries identified in chapter 1, with exact definitions of relevant SIC codes in appendix 1 of that chapter. Appendix 2 of chapter 1 shows the names of listed companies in each industry. 14 companies are listed under water transportation in that appendix, while 28 are considered here. The reason for that was explained in chapter 1, and it amounts to dropping companies from the industry which were listed under more than one SIC code.

In addition to returns, data have been collected from Datastream for each company in every industry to form the set of microeconomic variables entering equation (3.1). That is, data are collected for market values of equity, ME_{ijt}; earnings, needed to form the earnings-price ratios, E/P_{ijt}; Book Values of Equity, to form the Book to Market ratios, BE/ME_{ijt}; company asset values, to form the Asset to market ratios, A/ME_{ijt}; and the Asset to Book ratios, A/BE_{ijt}, all used in equation (3.1).

Finally, data on US macroeconomic variables entering equation (3.1) are collected from the same source. The variables required in equation (3.1) are: unanticipated changes in monthly industrial production, $UMIP_t$; unanticipated changes in monthly inflation, UI_t; unanticipated changes in the term structure of interest rates, UTS_t; unanticipated changes in oil prices, UOG_t; and unanticipated changes in consumption, UCG_t. It is argued that in efficiently operating markets, such as those in the US, anticipated changes in variables are foreseen and premia are discounted instantly. So the unanticipated changes in these macroeconomic variables are the relevant ones to enter in empirical estimation (see for e.g. Poon and Taylor, 1991). These are derived as follows:

1. The basic underlying data are identified,
2. The desired series is constructed,
3. ARIMA models are used to filter out the anticipated component of each series, and the unanticipated part – that is, the residual of the estimated ARIMA model – is used for estimation, provided the original series is not white noise.

Table 3.1, panel A, deals with the first step mentioned above. It sets the notation of the basic underlying data and its definition. Likewise, panel B focuses on the notation and the definition of the desired series constructed under step 2.

Since only the innovations or unanticipated changes in the macroeconomic variables are of interest, ARIMA models are used to filter out the anticipated component of each series

[2] However, at year-end 1994 the number of water transportation companies listed in the NY stock exchange had increased to approximately 40.

with 'memory'. Standard 20th order Box-Pierce Q-statistics[3] and autocorrelation coefficients calculated for the stock market index and each of the five series in panel B of table 3.1 (to test for serial correlation) are presented in table 3.2. As can be seen, the term structure (TS), oil prices (OG), consumption prices (CG) and inflation (I) are serially correlated. The excess market returns (XR_M) and monthly growth rate in industrial production (MIP) appear to be noisy enough to be treated as pure innovations.[4]

Table 3.1: Glossary and Definition of Macroeconomic Variables and Tranformations

PANEL A: Basic Series (Source - DataStream)

SYMBOL	DEFINITION
R_F	One month Treasury Bill
R_M	One month return on the S&P500 Composite Index
IP	Industrial Production during the month
LGB	End of period return on long - term Government bonds
CPI	US Consumer Price Index
O	Monthly Oil Brent price index
C	Monthly US Consumption

PANEL B: Derived Series

SYMBOL	DEFINITION
XR_M (=R_M - R_F)	One month excess return on the S&P500 Composite Index
MIP (monthly growth in IP)	Log relative of monthly IP
I (inflation)	Log relative of monthly CPI
TS (term structure)	LGB minus R_f
OG (oil price changes)	Log relative of monthly O
CG (consumption changes)	Log relative of monthly C

Based on investigation of the autocorrelations of TS, OG, CG, and I, and on Akaike (1973) and Schwarz (1978) information criteria, the 'best' ARMA model for each series is selected. The residuals from the fitted processes are used to proxy the unanticipated changes in these series. The new variables created in this way are: UTS, UOG, UCG, and

[3] See chapter 2 for details of these as well as a short discussion on ARIMA models.

[4] Note that we still denote the MIP as UMIP in the estimated models of the type shown in equation (3.1) as variations in the MIP series seem to be unanticipated.

UI. Autocorrelations and Q-statistics associated with these four variables, shown in table 3.2, reveal that there is no systematic part left in the 'news' series.

Table 3.2: Autocorrelation Coefficients and Unit Root Tests

Lags	XR_M	MIP	TS	OG	CG	I		UTS	UOG	UCG	UI
1	-0.25	0.104	0.927**	0.169	-0.062	0.365**		-0.083	-0.024	0.12	0.097
2	0.08	0.043	0.879**	-0.06	-0.166	0.058		0.014	-0.046	-0.092	-0.041
3	-0.091	0.19	0.836**	-0.008	0.416**	-0.068		0.013	0.003	-0.054	-0.125
4	0.151	0.036	0.784**	-0.001	-0.113	-0.009		0.049	0.048	0.007	0.025
5	-0.056	-0.024	0.740**	-0.278**	-0.125	0.099		0.008	-0.007	0.032	0.088
6	0.007	-0.162	0.705**	-0.295**	0.362**	-0.006		-0.011	-0.092	0.001	0.056
7	0.028	-0.009	0.632**	-0.055	-0.068	0.273**		-0.104	-0.058	0.11	0.025
8	0.104	0.034	0.590**	0.035	-0.081	0.184		0.071	0.049	-0.036	-0.004
9	0.035	-0.123	0.553**	-0.009	0.505**	0.024		0.016	-0.059	-0.055	-0.14
10	0.032	0.142	0.498**	0.006	-0.15	-0.011		0.033	-0.127	-0.013	0.018
11	0.111	0.082	0.446**	0.083	-0.163	-0.081		0.014	0.028	-0.046	-0.107
12	-0.052	0.035	0.403**	-0.037	0.326**	-0.081		0.014	0.028	-0.046	-0.107
Q (20)	20.5	21.1	768**	36.8**	141**	43.2**		12.5	11.9	10.6	19.2
ADF test	-8.595	-9.679	-8.896	-12.682	-9.527	-9.401		-10.768	-11.387	-10.13	-11.02
ADF lag	0	3	0	2	2	6		0	0	0	0

Notes: 1. Variables examined in the table are: Excess market returns (XR_M), monthly growth rate in industrial production (MIP), term structure (TS), oil prices (OG), consumption prices (CG), inflation (I), unanticipated changes in monthly inflation (UI), unanticipated changes in the term structure of interest rates (UTS), unanticipated changes in oil prices (UOG), unanticipated changes in consumption (UCG). 2. ** indicate significance at the 5% level. 3. ADF is the Augmented Dickey Fuller, testing for a unit root of the variable in question. 4. ADF lags for the unit root tests have been selected according to SBIC 4: 95% critical values for ADF statistics are –3.4484 for XR_M, MIP, TS, OG, CG and I, and -3.4527 for UTS, UOG, UCG, UI, respectively.

It is worth pointing here that all the macroeconomic series (whether filtered to create unanticipated components or not) investigated are stationary. This is verified using Augmented Dickey Fuller (ADF) tests, the values of which appear in table 3.2. The optimal lag structure in the ADF regression, shown in the same table, is chosen using the Schwarz Bayesian Information Criterion (SBIC). Thus, there is no need to difference the series before fitting the ARMA models to produce the unanticipated component of each series. It is important for the investigated series to be stationary, both when specifying the ARMA models and models of the type appearing in equation (3.1), in order to ensure that inferences are valid, see for instance Banerjee et al (1993) and chapter 2 of this book.

3.2.1 Correlation Amongst Variables

Table 3.3 displays the contemporaneous correlation coefficients among the relevant macroeconomic variables used in equation (3.1). Many, but not all, correlations are relatively small. The largest, -0.408, is between unanticipated inflation, UI and unanticipated consumption, UCG. The unanticipated change in consumption is also correlated with UTS, UOG and UMIP. According to Chen, Roll and Ross (1986) a significant correlation between the market index and some of the macroeconomic variables is to be expected since the market index should reflect information contained in the various series to the extent that they are important determinants of asset values. As can be seen, the excess market index return (XR_M) is significantly correlated with UMIP and UIP. Finally, UTS is correlated with UMIP, and UOG is correlated with UI. Nevertheless, table 3.3 suggests that the macrovariables employed in this study are far from perfectly correlated, and none of the variables can be readily replaced with any other.

Table 3.3: Correlation Matrix for Economic Variables

Variable	UTS	UOG	UCG	XR_M	UMIP	UI
UTS	1					
UOG	0.078	1				
UCG	0.204	** -0.33	** 1			
XR_M	-0.094	0.071	0.111	1		
UMIP	0.326	** -0.014	0.235	** -0.244	** 1	
UI	0.043	0.226	** -0.408	** -0.216	** 0.062	1

Notes: 1. See notes on table 3.2 for definition of variables. 2. ** indicates significance at the 5% level.

These results also go some way towards alleviating concerns about multicollinearity between the explanatory variables in models of the type appearing in equation (3.1).

3.3 Properties of Returns of the Water Transportation Industry

As a prelude to the analysis in subsequent chapters and to give some idea to the reader of the properties of the data on company returns, table 3.4 shows summary statistics of the monthly returns (shown in % terms here) for the water transportation industry over the period January 1985 to December 1994. During this period the shipping industry entered a phase of recovery starting in 1986 with freight rates, newbuilding and second hand prices shooting up, reaching a high plateau in the early nineties and falling subsequently. The post eighties era then, has seen the industry go through typical cycles of peaks and troughs. It is this eventful period, typical of the industry, that we analyze, and it comprises both conditions of high freight rates and prices and market downturns; that is, both bull and bear market conditions.

Table 3.4: Summary Statistics for % Monthly Returns over the period Jan 1985 - Dec 1994

Company	Mean %	Standard Deviation, %	Skewness	Excess Kurtosis	Coeff. Of Variation	ADF(1)
Alco Standard	1.38	6.81	-0.7179	2.0821	4.9228	-8.0557
Alexander and Baldwin	0.81	7.66	-0.2865	3.2297	9.4516	-8.4277
Amerada Hess	0.61	7.50	-0.3467	0.4166	12.3216	-7.1045
American President	0.85	12.16	-0.6518	0.8102	14.3733	-7.1464
Cincinnati Bell	1.38	6.95	0.0078	0.8265	5.0430	-6.9188
CSX	1.22	7.82	-1.3020	5.8769	6.4047	-8.7350
Eastern Enterprises	0.42	6.47	-0.6507	3.3888	15.3612	-9.4012
Exxon	1.26	4.53	-0.0039	2.9241	3.6040	-7.8536
GATX	1.09	8.05	-0.4917	2.2543	7.3752	-7.4487
Hawaiian Elec.Ind.	0.88	4.82	0.0645	-0.0261	5.4623	-7.6552
Hornbeck Offshore	1.78	21.21	0.8418	3.0669	11.8901	-5.9536
Interlake	-0.26	13.48	0.1722	1.1720	-51.3294	-7.8102
International Shipholding	1.51	8.72	0.3709	1.5838	5.7611	-7.4017
Lowe's Cos	1.66	11.60	-0.8617	2.9950	6.9964	-7.2195
Lynch	1.13	11.37	-0.7693	7.4472	10.0802	-7.1919
Mobil	1.34	5.22	-0.3739	2.0238	3.8916	-8.2310
Nicor	0.96	5.94	-0.5780	1.4613	6.1972	-7.9638
Offshore Logistics	1.43	18.68	1.2877	8.5006	13.0577	-7.8956
Oglebay Norton	0.55	7.56	-0.9583	6.6666	13.7046	-7.0028
OMI Corporation	0.74	11.88	-0.3221	0.8477	16.0878	-7.2578
Overseas Shipholding Group	0.81	9.03	-0.5667	0.6861	11.1570	-7.5622
Puget Sound Freight Lines	1.10	4.86	0.3409	2.3518	4.4371	-7.7697
Seaboard	1.12	9.21	0.1746	1.5888	8.2186	-6.3101
Sun	0.54	6.64	0.0096	-0.2210	12.4167	-8.3110
Teco Energy	1.30	4.41	-0.4657	0.3499	3.3924	-8.0254
Texaco	0.96	6.18	-0.1669	1.1496	6.4211	-7.7292
Tidewater	0.19	12.78	-0.6749	1.4377	66.9453	-8.1880
Van Ommeren	0.83	8.16	-1.0254	3.9443	9.8585	-7.2074
Average	**0.99**	**8.92**	**-0.2837**	**2.4584**	**8.6966**	
One Month Treasury Bill, R_f	0.46	1.75	-0.0353	-1.2285	3.8224	
S&P500 Return, R_{Mt}	0.85	4.37	-1.6627	8.9718	5.1698	-8.1198

Note: ADF(1) indicates the Augmented Dickey Fuller test, with 1 lag in the equation. The 5% critical value for the ADF test is -3.4481.

Considering the numbers in table 3.4 we observe that, with the exception of Interlake the water transportation companies' mean monthly returns are positive, while their industry average is 0.99% per month. This average monthly return is higher than the corresponding returns of the S&P500 market index and of the monthly US treasury bill rate (i.e. the risk free rate), which are 0.85% and 0.46%, respectively. Total average risk in the industry, as measured by the average standard deviation of monthly returns, is 8.92%, which is approximately twice as high as the 4.37% value of the S&P500 market index returns and approximately 5 times higher than the 1.75% return of the risk free rate. Dividing these standard deviations of returns with their own mean values provides a relative measure of riskiness, known as the coefficient of variation. These are 8.70%, 5.17% and 3.82% for the water transportation industry, the S&P500 return and the treasury bill rate, respectively. According to these results then the water transportation industry carries a risk which is higher than the average in the market. Theory would lead us to expect that higher returns than the market average would be expected to be earned by investors in the industry to compensate for this higher risk.

Coefficients of skewness are on average negative but not significantly different from zero, while there is significant positive excess kurtosis in the industry and the S&P500 market index, a result typical of most high frequency financial variables. Finally, first order ADF tests confirm that the water transportation companies and the S&P500 monthly returns are stationary. As a result regressing company on market returns and other variables, as in equation (3.1), produces meaningful results and inferences from such models are valid (see for e.g. Engle and Granger, 1987).

Should the above results regarding the total risk – return comparisons be used however, as indications of risk carried by water transportation companies? The financial literature, following the introduction of the Capital Asset Pricing Model (CAPM) by Sharpe(1964) and Lintner(1965), asserts that the total asset risk (the standard deviation) of a stock may be split into a systematic (non-diversifiable) risk, and a non-systematic (diversifiable) risk. This is a significant result since, as an investor can eliminate the effects of non-systematic risk by suitably diversifying his/her portfolio across stocks, one needs only consider the systematic - non-diversifiable or market risk - to decide on the risk involved in holding a stock. This market specific risk of a company is known as its beta, and is the subject matter of subsequent chapters in the book.

3.4 Conclusion

The aim of this chapter has been to discuss sources of data and variable transformations required to perform the analysis in later chapters in the book. It has identified Datastream International as the data source that can provide information on all the variables required for estimation of the empirical models. The necessary data transformations have been performed, and the properties of the variables have been examined. In addition, the properties of stock returns of companies listed in the water transportation industry are considered. These properties indicate that the risk profile of the industry is higher than the market requiring higher returns than the market to compensate. It is argued that as total risk can be separated into diversifiable and non-diversifiable risk, through the formation of portfolios, it is more appropriate to consider non-diversifiable measures of risk as the relevant metric for comparison. This is the subject matter of the analysis in the rest of the book.

CHAPTER 4: RESULTS FROM THE CAPM – CAPITAL ASSET PRICING MODEL

4.1. Introduction

The Capital Asset Pricing Model (CAPM) is employed in this chapter to determine whether the systematic risk of the water transportation industry is different from that of the "average" company in the market, and to consider whether risk has changed over time and also under different market conditions (bull and bear market conditions). The systematic risk is identified to be the appropriate measure of risk and its advantages over the use of total risk are highlighted.

It would be of interest to potential investors in the water transportation industry, whose aim is to build diversified portfolios of assets, to know how this industry fared among other industries, in terms of its risk-return characteristics over time and over economic cycles. It is often feared that the high volatility of the industry with its sharp ups and downs acts negatively upon potential investors.

Also consideration of differing risks in the industry over varying economic conditions is important in portfolio selection, since as Levy (1974) suggests portfolios with high betas will outperform "averages" over bull market conditions and portfolios with low betas will successfully resist bear market conditions. That is, betas will be positively correlated with returns in a bull market and negatively correlated in a bear market. Separate beta coefficients for bull and bear markets may then be calculated and select stocks and portfolios according to these.

The second issue addressed in this chapter also employs the CAPM to analyse the stock returns of the water transportation industry along with the returns of seven other industries, air transportation, trucks, rail transportation, electricity, gas, petroleum refining and real estate. The aim of this analysis is to compare systematic risk across industries through the comparison of industry betas. The findings of this chapter suggest that the water transportation industry exhibits lower market risk than the "average" stock and the rail transportation industry, higher market risk than the real estate industry and similar market risk to the remaining industries analysed.

4.2. The Capital Asset Pricing Model (CAPM) and Market Risk

According to the CAPM of Sharpe (1964) and Lintner (1965), the expected return on a firm's equity can be explained as a linear function of a single factor, namely, the expected return on the market portfolio of assets. In empirical work regarding the CAPM, the proxy for this market return is taken to represent a broad measure of stock market returns (such as the S&P 500). The model splits asset risk into two components. The first known as market or systematic risk, represents that portion of asset risk that is related to the riskiness of the market portfolio. The second component is known as residual, or nonsystematic risk and is the portion of total asset risk that is company specific, and unrelated to the market portfolio. Because an investor can eliminate the effects of residual risk by suitably diversifying his portfolio, the implication from the CAPM is that the expected returns on individual assets should reflect only their systematic risk. The above ideas are summarised in equation 1:

$$XR_{jt} = \alpha_j + \beta_j XR_{Mt} + \varepsilon_{jt} \tag{4.1}$$

where XR_{jt} is the expected excess[1] holding period return on the equity of shipping company j in period t, XR_{Mt} is the expected excess holding period return on the market portfolio of stocks in period t, and ε_{jt} is the residual left unexplained by the regression of the expected return on the market portfolio, the nonsystematic risk.

β_j and α_j are the parameters of the CAPM, which may be estimated using OLS regression methods discussed in chapter 2. The former measures the sensitivity of the stock of shipping company j to changes in the expected return on the market portfolio, while the latter indicates deviations from equilibrium pricing; if it is positive it implies that the stock is underpriced and if it is negative that the stock is overpriced. The CAPM suggests that an average stock in the market portfolio would have a beta value of one. An asset with β_j greater (lower) than unity carries above (below) "average" systematic risk, and investors would therefore require higher (lower) expected return to hold it.

[1] All holding period returns are expressed in excess of the risk-free rate of return, where that rate is the yield on a short-term treasury bill. All stock prices and cash dividends have been adjusted for stock splits and stock dividends.

Equation (4.1) is estimated, by OLS, for each water transportation company for the entire period. Alpha and beta estimates from these time series regressions are then used to establish average alpha and beta values for the shipping sector and standard cross sectional t tests, test whether they are significantly different from zero and one respectively (see chapter 2 for details on the technicalities).

A problem which may arise with the time series estimates of alpha and beta is that these may be non constant over time. To allow for that, equation (4.1) is estimated for each half sample period for every company and standard Chow tests on individual companies and of the industry average are used to determine the stability of the parameters of each company and the whole industry.

4.2.1. The CAPM under different market conditions

The constancy of alphas and betas of each company over bull and bear markets is also investigated. Equation (4.1) is thus augmented to equation (4.2) to include the binary variable d_t which takes the value of unity in bull market conditions and zero otherwise.

$$\mathbf{XR}_{jt} = \alpha_{1j} + \alpha_{2j}\mathbf{d}_t + \beta_{1j}\mathbf{XR}_{Mt} + \beta_{2j}(\mathbf{d}_t\mathbf{XR}_{Mt}) + \varepsilon_{jt} \qquad (4.2)$$

The coefficients of the binary variables α_{2j} and β_{2j} measure the differential effects of bull over bearish market conditions on the alpha, α_{1j}, and beta, β_{1j}, for the jth stock. Thus under bearish market conditions, equation 2 reduces to the simple CAPM (equation (4.1)) because $\alpha_{2j}d_t = \beta_{2j}d_tXR_{Mt} = 0$. Therefore, if the alpha and/or beta for the jth stock differ over bull and bear markets then α_{2j} and/or β_{2j} will be significantly different from zero.

The definition of bull and bear markets is of paramount importance in this test. We adopt two definitions proposed in a related context by Fabozzi and Francis (1977). Bull market months are defined as those months in which the market return, R_{Mt}, is positive and bear market months those in which the market return, R_{Mt}, is negative. This procedure yields a mutually exclusive and exhaustive division of the total sample of 120 months into two subsets. In an alternative definition, three sets of months are distinguished: - a) months when the market moved up substantially, b) months when the market moved down substantially and c) months when the market moved neither up or down substantially. Months included in categories a) and b) are those months in which the absolute value of R_{Mt} is larger than half of one standard deviation of the market's returns measured over the total period, that is:

$$| R_{Mt}| > 0.5\sigma_{Mt} \quad (4.3)$$

Months which do not fulfill this condition fall under category c) and are ignored since the market is deemed to be directionless under the criterion of equation (4.3).

4.3. Results for the Water Transportation Industry

Two samples are utilised for the purposes of this chapter. One with 28 companies, which concentrates on water transportation stocks, is used to analyse and compare the industry with the market, over time and under different market conditions. The other one, of 14 listed companies, is used to produce results which enable comparison between the water transportation industry and other industries. The set of 14 listed stocks is a subset of the above set of 28, and excludes companies which are also listed under other industries. The reason for that is to produce a relatively more pure set of estimates for alphas and betas, which are not distorted by estimates of companies which are diversified into more than one of the industries analysed in this book.

The availability of water-transportation stocks in the stock exchange facilitates analysis of risk return profiles of the industry, comparison with typical market returns and comparison with these characteristics of other industries. This information would aid the decision making process of fund managers who are faced with choices of stocks to select for portfolio formation from a number of industries. While other industry specific studies have appeared in the finance literature,[2] there has been no evidence on the water transportation or other transportation industries. This work aims to address this gap in the literature.

[2] See for example Neuberger (1991) and Kane and Unal (1988) who focus on the risk returns characteristics of the US banking sector, and Gyourko and Keim (1993) who consider the real estate industry in the US.

4.3.1. Comparison of the Industry with the Market Index

Results of the CAPM (as expressed in equation (4.1)), estimated for each of the 28 water transportation stocks over the entire period and the two subperiods, are in tables 4.2.A, 4.2.B and 4.2.C, respectively. Average values of the industry parameters on alphas and betas, derived at the last rows of these tables, are summarised in table 4.1:

Table 4.1: CAPM Estimates Across Companies

Estimated Period	Alpha	Beta	Adjusted R-square	Standard Error of Regression
Whole Period Jan 85 - Dec 94	0.0021 * (0.0011)	0.9199 *** (0.0741)	0.2324	0.0785
Sub - Period 1: Jan 85 - Dec 89	0.0043 ** (0.0018)	0.9018 *** (0.0744)	0.2793	0.0836
Sub - Period 2: Jan 90 - Dec 94	0.0000 (0.0019)	0.9507 *** (0.1055)	0.1724	0.0663

Notes: 1. ***, ** and * indicate significance at the 1%, 5% and 10%, respectively. 2. Standard errors are in brackets. 3. See chapter 2 for details of how these statistics are derived.

Over the whole period, all betas are statistically significant at conventional significance levels and range in value from 0.288 to 1.699 with a mean value of 0.9199. Alphas are mostly insignificant with the exception of Teco Energy, Amerada Hess and Lowe's Cos, and range from -0.008 to 0.011 with a mean value of 0.0021.

Over the first subperiod, as can be seen in table 4.2.B, all betas are statistically significant at conventional levels of significance and range in value from 0.216 to 1.845 with a mean value of 0.9018. Alphas are again mostly insignificant with the exception of Teco Energy, Hawaiian Elec.Ind., Puget Sound Freight Lines, Amerada Hess and Cincinnati Bell and range in value from -0.0194 to 0.0251 with a mean value of 0.0043.

Over the second subperiod, as can be seen in table 4.2.C, the majority of betas are statistically significant. The only exceptions are International Shipholding, Interlake and Hornbeck Offshore. During this period betas range in value from 0.189 to 2.759 with a mean value of 0.951 which is slightly higher than the corresponding value of the first subperiod. All alphas are statistically insignificant during this period thus indicating "fair" pricing of the stocks. They range in value from -0.0393 to 0.0189, the average being substantially lower than in the first subperiod standing at zero.

The (average) industry beta, as can be seen in table 4.1 is different from zero at all levels of significance for the whole period and the two subperiods. Alpha is positive but not significant at conventional significance levels for the second period, significant at the 5% level for the first subperiod and significant at the 10% level for the whole period.

Table 4.2.A: CAPM estimates and statistics for the period Jan. 85 - Dec. 94

Company	Alpha	Beta	Adjusted R-square	Standard Error of Regression	DW	Chow test
Alco Standard	0.0046	1.0911 ***	0.4865	0.0488	2.1291	0.4811
Alexander and Baldwin	0.0009	0.8509 ***	0.2292	0.0672	2.1499	1.1489
Amerada Hess	0.0002 **	0.6982 ***	0.1582	0.0688	1.5916	0.2401
American President	-0.0049	1.5844 ***	0.3186	0.1003	2.1638	6.5260 **
Cincinnati Bell	0.0077	0.7208 ***	0.1988	0.0622	1.5693	4.6347 **
CSX	0.0008	1.3448 ***	0.5611	0.0518	2.1178	1.3330
Eastern Enterprises	-0.0034	0.8950 ***	0.3606	0.0517	2.0858	0.0009
Exxon	0.0072	0.6403 ***	0.3755	0.0358	2.0706	0.5249
GATX	0.0021	1.0476 ***	0.3176	0.0665	1.7293	1.7844
Hawaiian Elec.Ind.	0.0053	0.4160 ***	0.1349	0.0448	2.0306	1.6232
Hornbeck Offshore	0.0104	0.8763 **	0.0244	0.2094	1.7680	0.0049
Interlake	-0.0121	1.1235 ***	0.1254	0.1260	2.0856	3.1098
International Shipholding	0.0100	0.6110 ***	0.0862	0.0833	1.8310	2.1461
Lowe's Cos	0.0047 *	1.4029 ***	0.2733	0.0989	2.1061	3.8062 **
Lynch	-0.0031	1.6990 ***	0.4211	0.0865	1.7322	0.9256
Mobil	0.0076	0.6825 ***	0.3209	0.0430	1.8920	0.0523
Nicor	0.0058	0.4515 ***	0.1028	0.0563	2.0517	0.0970
Offshore Logistics	0.0009	1.5822 ***	0.1296	0.1743	2.2007	0.0138
Oglebay Norton	-0.0028	0.9853 ***	0.3188	0.0624	1.7748	3.2248
OMI Corporation	-0.0051	1.4800 ***	0.2905	0.1001	1.9359	0.3245
Overseas Shipholding Group	-0.0015	1.1386 ***	0.2979	0.0756	2.0593	0.0886
Puget Sound Freight Lines	0.0064	0.5406 ***	0.2295	0.0427	1.9662	0.4509
Seaboard	0.0065	0.5597 ***	0.0627	0.0891	2.0006	0.1014
Sun	-0.0007	0.7184 ***	0.2168	0.0588	2.2540	1.5788
Teco Energy	0.0106 ***	0.2888 ***	0.0739	0.0425	2.0384	0.9452
Texaco	0.0053	0.5135 ***	0.1246	0.0578	2.1833	0.0400
Tidewater	-0.0078	1.1471 ***	0.1466	0.1181	1.8309	0.5168
Van Ommeren	0.0026	0.6662 ***	0.1199	0.0765	2.0482	0.2398
Industry Average	**0.0021 ***	**0.9199 *****	**0.2324**	**0.0785**	**1.9785**	**1.1200**

Notes: ***, ** and * indicate significance at the 1%, 5% and 10%, respectively.

As mentioned in the preceding paragraphs the average beta for the whole period is 0.920, and 0.902 and 0.951 for the two subperiods. This beta, is insignificantly less than one, the market beta, at the 10% level of significance, for the first five year subperiod, while, it is not significantly less than one for the whole and second periods. The non-significant value of alpha for the second subperiod suggests that, on average, the sample of water transportation company stocks was priced correctly during this period. Evidence of underpricing occurs in the whole period and in the first five-year subperiod where the alpha is positive and significant. However, it should be noted that the industry alpha's statistical significance during the first subperiod is due to an outlier, the very high value of the alpha of Cincinnati Bell. When this outlier is excluded from the cross-sectional tests, the industry alpha becomes insignificant during the first subperiod too.

Table 4.2.B: CAPM estimates and statistics for the period Jan. 85 - Dec. 89

Company	Alpha		Beta		Standard Error of Regression	Adjusted R-square	DW
Alco Standard	0.0025		1.1534	***	0.0480	0.6149	2.5560
Alexander and Baldwin	0.0087		0.8900	***	0.0767	0.2622	2.2007
Amerada Hess	0.0019	*	0.7456	***	0.0745	0.2064	1.4762
American President	-0.0066		1.1629	***	0.0948	0.2852	2.1573
Cincinnati Bell	0.0251	***	0.6236	***	0.0619	0.2087	1.6725
CSX	-0.0067		1.3429	***	0.0540	0.6286	2.1945
Eastern Enterprises	-0.0036		0.8958	***	0.0456	0.5127	1.9573
Exxon	0.0093		0.6664	***	0.0400	0.4293	2.2152
GATX	0.0044		0.8853	***	0.0594	0.3740	1.8454
Hawaiian Elec.Ind.	0.0116	*	0.3312	***	0.0494	0.0969	2.0892
Hornbeck Offshore	0.0122		0.8792	***	0.2680	0.0126	1.7935
Interlake	0.0161		1.1009	***	0.0765	0.3571	1.6400
International Shipholding	0.0198		0.7342	***	0.0929	0.1347	1.6455
Lowe's Cos	-0.0097		1.1970	***	0.0699	0.4425	2.0869
Lynch	-0.0030		1.8448	***	0.0983	0.4893	1.6354
Mobil	0.0083		0.6941	***	0.0482	0.3576	1.8257
Nicor	0.0081		0.4452	***	0.0612	0.1146	2.0829
Offshore Logistics	0.0009		1.6185	***	0.2306	0.1066	2.2089
Oglebay Norton	-0.0053		1.1866	***	0.0625	0.4952	1.8772
OMI Corporation	0.0024		1.4646	***	0.1089	0.3261	1.9240
Overseas Shipholding Group	0.0011		1.1070	***	0.0769	0.3576	2.2225
Puget Sound Freight Lines	0.0100	*	0.5435	***	0.0451	0.2778	2.1266
Seaboard	0.0098		0.5190	***	0.1035	0.0500	1.8925
Sun	0.0036		0.5829	***	0.0609	0.1914	2.5659
Teco Energy	0.0139	**	0.2156	**	0.0451	0.0444	2.1714
Texaco	0.0068		0.5100	***	0.0725	0.1070	2.1380
Tidewater	-0.0192		1.1983	***	0.1357	0.1658	1.7253
Van Ommeren	-0.0020		0.7129	***	0.0795	0.1704	1.9362
Industry Average	**0.0043**	**	**0.9018**	***	**0.0836**	**0.2793**	**1.9951**

Notes: ***, ** and * indicate significance at the 1%, 5% and 10%, respectively.

Furthermore, the industry alpha's statistical significance at the 10% level for the whole period is also due to three outliers; Teco Energy, International Shipholding, and Hornbeck

Offshore. Excluding these from the cross-sectional test results produces an insignificant alpha.

Table 4.2.C: CAPM estimates and statistics for the period Jan.90 - Dec.94.

Company	Alpha	Beta		Standard Error of Regression	Adjusted R-square	DW
Alco Standard	0.0066	0.9376	***	0.0502	0.2583	1.8646
Alexander and Baldwin	-0.0067	0.6773	***	0.0560	0.1199	2.1462
Amerada Hess	-0.0015	0.5532	**	0.0637	0.0584	1.8195
American President	-0.0027	2.7594	***	0.0970	0.4531	2.0080
Cincinnati Bell	-0.0090	0.8419	***	0.0587	0.1652	1.6607
CSX	0.0081	1.4135	***	0.0492	0.4586	2.0846
Eastern Enterprises	-0.0032	0.8949	***	0.0580	0.1885	2.1371
Exxon	0.0050	0.5500	***	0.0315	0.2323	1.9583
GATX	0.0000	1.4749	***	0.0721	0.2961	1.6046
Hawaiian Elec.Ind.	-0.0007	0.5965	***	0.0392	0.1837	1.9556
Hornbeck Offshore	0.0087	0.8533		0.1315	0.0263	1.6476
Interlake	-0.0393	0.9482		0.0580	0.1575	2.1448
International Shipholding	0.0003	0.1885		0.0706	-0.0096	2.2051
Lowe's Cos	0.0189	2.0915	***	0.1173	0.2397	2.3893
Lynch	-0.0033	1.2970	***	0.0731	0.2381	1.8859
Mobil	0.0070	0.6445	***	0.0379	0.2225	1.9875
Nicor	0.0035	0.4490	**	0.0518	0.0581	1.9176
Offshore Logistics	0.0009	1.4825	***	0.0928	0.1999	1.9396
Oglebay Norton	-0.0007	0.4518	*	0.0599	0.0407	1.8377
OMI Corporation	-0.0124	1.4588	***	0.0917	0.1986	1.9506
Overseas Shipholding Group	-0.0041	1.2032	***	0.0755	0.1989	1.8806
Puget Sound Freight Lines	0.0029	0.5024	***	0.0405	0.1256	1.7836
Seaboard	0.0033	0.6441	**	0.0737	0.0592	2.1784
Sun	-0.0047	1.0549	***	0.0560	0.2615	1.9895
Teco Energy	0.0075	0.4621	***	0.0398	0.1105	1.8213
Texaco	0.0038	0.5102	***	0.0391	0.1387	2.3834
Tidewater	0.0032	1.1023	***	0.0984	0.1026	2.0935
Van Ommeren	0.0071	0.5769	**	0.0745	0.0438	2.1466
Industry Average	**0.0000**	**0.9507**	***	**0.0663**	**0.1724**	**1.9793**

Notes: ***, ** and * indicate significance at the 1%, 5% and 10%, respectively.

Chow tests, presented in table 4.2.A, test for the joint stability of the regression coefficients over the two sub periods conducted for each company and indicate that in 25 out of the 28 companies in our sample, equation (4.1) is stable over time. Furthermore, a Chow test at the aggregate industry level confirms the relationship to be stable.

Use of the CAPM has also allowed decomposition of total risk into systematic and non-systematic risks. The systematic risk of the industry then as measured by beta is equal, if not lower, than the average stock. The model explains only about 23 percent of the total variation of returns during the whole sample period. This means that returns in the industry contained a large portion of nonsystematic risk. Investors may diversify this risk by appropriately weighting water transportation stocks in a portfolio consisting of stocks from other industries whose performance is negatively correlated to that of the water transportation industry.

4.3.2. Bull Versus Bear Market Conditions

Results regarding the variation of the distribution of returns of shipping companies over bull and bear markets are also presented. Both definitions of bull/bear market conditions suggested in section 4.2 are used to estimate equations 4.1 and 4.2. An F-test on the incremental sum of squares, obtained by advancing from equation (4.1) to equation (4.2), is used to determine if the alpha and beta changed significantly between bull and bear market conditions. The results of this test at the 5% level of statistical significance, reported in table 4.3.A, indicate that the CAPM yields significantly different estimates of alpha and beta for 5 out of 28 (17.86%) companies under definition 1, and for 2 (7.14%) companies under definition 2, over bull and bear markets.

Table 4.3.A: Summary Statistics for Equation (4.2), estimated over 28 stocks

Bull and Bear Definitions (observations)	Significance Test [c]	Number of Companies (proportion, %, in brackets)	Test Statistic for proportion: Π=0
Definition 1 [a] (120 observations)	α_{2j} and $\beta_{2j} \neq 0$	5 (17.86%)	2.47 sig
Definition 2 [b] (63 observations)	α_{2j} and $\beta_{2j} \neq 0$	2 (7.14%)	1.47 insig

Notes: a : Bull Market: $R_{Mt} > 0$, b: Bull Market: $R_{Mt} > 0.5\sigma_M$, c : F-test on the joint significance of α_{2j} and β_{2j} in equation (4.2) (see chapter 2 for details), sig./insig.: Indicates statistical significance/insignificance of the percentage in brackets (see chapter 2 for details).

Table 4.3.B: Summary Statistics for Separate t-tests on Alphas and Betas

Bull and Bear Definition (observations)	Coefficient Tested [c]	Number of Companies (proportion, %, in brackets)	Test Statistic for proportion: Π=0
Definition 1 [a] (120 observations)	α_{2j}	4 (14.29%)	2.16 sig.
	β_{2j}	3 (10.71%)	1.83 insig.
Definition 2 [b] (63 observations)	α_{2j}	2 (7.14%)	1.47 insig.
	β_{2j}	1 (3.57%)	1.02 insig.

Notes: a : Bull Market: $R_{Mt} > 0$, b: Bull Market: $R_{Mt} > 0.5\sigma_M$, c : Two-tailed t-test. (see chapter 2 for details), sig./insig.: Indicates statistical significance/insignificance of the percentage in brackets (see chapter 2 for details).

Statistical tests, on the last column of the same table, test the significance of the above percentages (proportions). The first one indicates that 17.86% was significantly different from zero at the 5% level, which means that under definition 1 the CAPM yields different estimates of alpha and beta over bull and bear markets. The second test on the other hand indicates that 7.14% is not significant at the same level of significance, which means that, under definition 2, the CAPM does not yield different estimates of alpha and beta over bull and bear markets. Therefore, we can conclude that for normal market upturns/downturns (definition 1) the CAPM may yield different estimates of alpha and beta but this is not the case for larger market upturns/downturns (definition 2).

To determine if either the alpha or the beta coefficients were individually less stable over bull and bear markets the t-statistics of α_{2j} and β_{2j} in equation (4.2) for each of the 28 water transportation stocks were calculated and examined separately. If the jth stock's alpha or beta shifted significantly then the t-statistic for α_{2j} or β_{2j} would be significant. As can be seen in table 4.3.B the percentage of significant t-statistics in equation 2 is quite small. In fact, tests carried out for each percentage indicated instability over bull and bear markets only for the alpha under definition 1. This means that the change of market conditions from bullish to bearish does not cause systematic shifts in the beta under definitions 1 and 2 and the alpha under definition 2. Therefore, the shift in the equation suggested by the discussion in the preceding paragraph is due to the shift of the intercept of the equation, not the slope. As a result, investors need not worry about the riskiness of portfolios comprising water transportation stocks between bull and bear market conditions; there seem to be no significant differences in systematic risk, Levy (1974).

4.3.3. The Size Effect

Past studies [see e.g. Banz (1981) and Reinganum (1981, 1986)] find evidence of an inverse relationship between size and risk and average returns. To the best of our knowledge no previous study has investigated this relationship for the water transportation industry. However, Carleton and Lakonishok(1986) investigated the size anomaly over a number of industries including transportation. They find evidence of the size anomaly for the transportation industry as indeed for all the industries they include in their study. A priori one may therefore expect stocks of different sized water transportation companies to face differing sensitivities to risk and return factors. For example, investors may face higher transaction costs on small size water transportation companies than on large size ones; higher returns are required to compensate for such costs. However, the stock of a large water transportation company may reflect the company's enhanced opportunities for diversification or its capability to better exploit economies of scale in comparison to a smaller company. This would be reflected in the lower risk characteristics of its stock.

To test for such size effects, the 28 companies have been allocated to 4 size groups according to their market values in January 1985 and 1989, as in tables 4.3.C and 4.3.D. Group 1 contains the smallest companies while group 4 contains the largest. Summary statistics of average returns, total risk, alphas and betas are estimated.

Table 4.3.C: Summary Statistics according to Size (Period Jan.85-Dec.89)

Size (Market Value, MV, of Equity - millions US$)	No. of companies	Average MV	Average Returns	Average Std Deviation	Average Alpha	Average Beta
0-100	7	36.157	0.020	0.154	0.005	1.178
100-500	8	354.693	0.015	0.092	0.004	0.890
500-1000	7	717.221	0.014	0.066	0.004	0.763
1000-Over	6	11106.007	0.014	0.072	0.004	0.757

Notes: Group 1 (MV 0-100) consists of the following companies: Hornbeck, Offshore Logistics, Lynch, International Shipholding, OMI, Seaboard, Oglebay.
Group 2 (MV 100-500) consists of the following companies: Interlake, Van Ommeren, Hawaiian Electricity, Tidewater, Cincinatti Bell, OSG, GATX, American President.
Group 3 (MV 500-1000) consists of the following companies: Eastern Enterprises, Puget, Alco, Alexander and Baldwin, Nicor, Teco, Lowe's company.
Group 4 (MV 1000-over) consists of the following companies: Amerada, CSX, Sun, Texaco, Mobil, Exxon.

Table 4.3.D: Summary Statistics according to Size (Period Jan.89-Dec.94)

Size (MV of Equity – millions US$)	No. of companies	Average MV	Average Returns	Average Std Deviation	Average Alpha	Average Beta
0-100	4	60.705	0.001	0.087	0.004	0.698
100-500	5	223.908	-0.009	0.109	-0.004	1.127
500-1000	6	695.210	-0.001	0.081	0.005	1.251
1000-Over	13	9672.468	0.003	0.058	0.006	0.822

Notes: Group 1 (MV 0-100) consists of the following companies: Hornbeck, Lynch, Oglebay, International Shipholding.
Group 2 (MV 100-500) consists of the following companies: Interlake, Tidewater, Offshore Logistics, Seaboard, OMI.
Group 3 (MV 500-1000) consists of the following companies: Eastern Enterprises, Van Ommeren, American President, GATX, OSG, Hawaiian Electricity.
Group 4 (MV 1000-over) consists of the following companies: Amerada, CSX, Sun, Texaco, Mobil, Exxon, Lowe's company, Puget, Alco, Alexander and Baldwin, Nicor, Teco, Cincinnatti Bell.

In line with the findings of Banz (1981) and Reinganum (1981, 1986), small water transportation companies significantly outperform their larger counterparts in terms of average returns during the period 1985-1989. The average returns of medium sized and large companies do not seem to exhibit any significant differences. Also, higher returns of smaller companies are accompanied by significantly higher total and systematic risk. The average total risk - as measured by the standard deviation - of companies in the first group (the smaller ones) is twice that of the companies in the fourth group (the larger ones). Similarly, while the systematic risk - as measured by beta - of the smaller companies is 1.178 that of the larger companies is 0.757. Generally speaking during the period 1984-1989, considering all four groups of companies, there appears to be an inverse relationship between size and total and systematic risk. Smaller companies also exhibit the highest alphas, therefore the highest underpricing, compared to other sizes. Studies in the past, e.g. Keim (1983), Carleton and Lakonishok (1986) suggest that the "size effect" is concentrated mainly in the month of January. To test for this anomaly, we excluded the January returns of the companies in our sample during the period 1985-1989 and still found small water transportation companies to significantly outperform larger ones.

However, the relationships described above break down in the second time period of our study. While there is a substantial downward trend in the average returns of all four groups the previously documented excess returns of smaller companies totally disappears. Furthermore, their average total risk and betas have decreased substantially (almost halved). These risk parameters have increased for the medium sized companies whereas for the large companies they have stayed at more or less the same levels. Alphas have decreased for the first two groups and increased for the third and fourth groups. A closer look at tables 4.3.C and 4.3.D reveals that there have been noticeable changes in the frequencies of the four size deciles of our sample. While in the first subperiod there were seven small and fifteen medium sized companies, in the second subperiod they decreased to four and eleven respectively. In contrast, the number of large companies has more than doubled from the first to the second subperiod. This shift from "small" and "medium" towards "big" could well explain the differences in the results between the first and second subperiods of the study.

4.4. Comparison of the Water Transportation Beta with other Industries

Investors, when deciding on which industries to invest on, consider the risk return profiles of several industries. This section takes this idea on board to measure risk-return relationships in a number of other industries in the US economy and compare the performance of water transportation stocks with that of these other industries. Temporal analysis is also undertaken by subdividing the 11-year period into two equal subperiods: July 1984 to December 1989, and January 1990 to June 1995. Such analysis enables us to observe whether betas have changed over time for the water transportation and the other industries.

The CAPM then, as expressed in equation (4.1), is estimated across companies for each industry[3] as a multiequation system over the entire period and for the two subperiods. This is convenient since as was mentioned in Chapter 2 of this book, it allows the imposition of common equation constraints (e.g. of a single average β for each industry) during estimation.[4] The results of each industry's parameters are summarised in table 4.4.A.

All industries' average alphas are significantly positive for the whole period and the two subperiods, suggesting that on average the companies in the industries analysed are underpriced. The average alpha of the water transportation industry for the whole period (0.0352) and the second subperiod (0.0304) is lower than the average alpha of only two industries (gas, and petroleum refining), while its average alpha for the first subperiod (0.0371) is lower than that of three industries (electricity, gas, and petroleum refining).

The average beta of the water transportation industry for the full eleven-year period is 0.9411. Table 4.4.B tests whether each industry's systematic risk (its beta) is significantly different to that of the market. As can be seen, the average market betas of four industries (trucks, rail transportation, petroleum refining and air transportation) are not significantly different to the "average" market beta of unity, while the average market beta of the water transportation industry and three other industries (real estate, gas, and electricity) are significantly lower than unity, indicating below average systematic risk.

---

[3] Care has been taken to exclude companies from an industry, if according to the SIC classification, they are listed under more than one industries. In that way more representative values of alphas and betas are obtained for each industry. For instance, the number of companies listed under water transportation now are 14 rather than 28.

[4] SURE is often used for estimation of such simultaneous, multiequation models since it allows for the possibility of cross-equation correlation in the residuals, see for example Stambaugh (1982) and Gibbons (1982). It is reasonable to expect that the residuals of equation (4.1) would be correlated across stocks of the same industry. However, Theil (1971) has shown that in SURE systems when the explanatory variables are the same between equations, as in equation (4.1), then there is no gain in efficiency by using SURE and the result is equivalent to using OLS separately for each equation. One may still estimate the equations as a system in an MLSQ framework without adjusting for cross-equation correlation in the residuals using the usual ML methods. This is what we do in this case.

Table 4.4.A: CAPM Estimates across Industries

Panel A: CAPM results for each industry for the period July 1984 - June 1995

Industry	Intercept (alpha)		Systematic risk (beta)		R - Square
Water Transportation	0.0352	**	0.9411	**	0.6539
	(0.0018)		(0.0173)		
Air Transportation	0.0124	**	0.9748	**	0.7130
	(0.0026)		(0.0355)		
Rail Transportation	0.0150	**	1.0155	**	0.5918
	(0.0025)		(0.0333)		
Trucks	0.0206	**	0.9676	**	0.5328
	(0.0018)		(0.0308)		
Electricity	0.0668	**	0.9465	**	0.7130
	(0.0023)		(0.0097)		
Gas	0.0447	**	0.9581	**	0.6410
	(0.0017)		(0.0091)		
Petroleum Refining	0.0339	**	0.9838	**	0.5466
	(0.0024)		(0.0362)		
Real Estate	0.0260	**	0.6933	**	0.3526
	(0.0034)		(0.1294)		

Panel B: CAPM results for each industry for the period July 1984 - December 1989

Industry	Intercept (alpha)		Systematic risk (beta)		R – Square
Water Transportation	0.0371	**	0.9472	**	0.6074
	(0.0025)		(0.0173)		
Air Transportation	0.0137	**	0.9372	**	0.4729
	(0.0037)		(0. 0384)		
Rail Transportation	0.0169	**	0.9946	**	0.5510
	(0.0031)		(0.0606)		
Trucks	0.0175	**	0.9302	**	0.5356
	(0.0025)		(0.0548)		
Electricity	0.0749	**	0.9273	**	0.6457
	(0.0025)		(0.0137)		
Gas	0.0506	**	0.9525	**	0.6133
	(0.0033)		(0.0192)		
Petroleum Refining	0.0407	**	1.0290	**	0.5238
	(0.0037)		(0.0425)		
Real Estate	0.0227	**	0.7242	**	0.3156
	(0.0054)		(0.1296)		

Panel C: CAPM results for each industry for the period January 1990 - June 1995

Industry	Intercept (alpha)		Systematic risk (beta)		R – square
Water Transportation	0.0304	**	0.9402	**	0.7115
	(0.0023)		(0.0261)		
Air Transportation	0.0085	**	1.0085	**	0.5357
	(0.0028)		(0.0513)		
Rail Transportation	0.0164	**	1.0290	**	0.6355
	(0.0036)		(0.0250)		
Trucks	0.0200	**	1.0009	**	0.5759
	(0.0021)		(0.0273)		
Electricity	0.0597	**	0.9631	**	0.8048
	(0.0020)		(0.0127)		
Gas	0.0427	**	0.9598	**	0.6954
	(0.0018)		(0.0121)		
Petroleum Refining	0.0283	**	0.9480	**	0.6335
	(0.0027)		(0.0397)		
Real Estate	0.0266	**	0.6705	**	0.3999
	(0.0037)		(0.1434)		

Notes: 1. Figures in brackets are standard errors. 2. ** indicate significance at the 5% level. 3. See chapter 2 for details of how these statistics are derived.

The market beta of the water transportation industry during the first subperiod is 0.9473, while in the second subperiod it is 0.9402. The beta of the water transportation industry is significantly lower than unity for both subperiods along with the market betas of the real estate, the gas, and electricity industries. The betas of the remaining four industries are, as for the whole period, not significantly different to one.

Table 4.4.B: Tests of Equality of the Betas of each Industry and the Market Beta

Industry	*1984:7-1995:6*		*1984:7-1989:12*		*1990:1-1995:6*	
	t-statistic		*t-statistic*		*t-statistic*	
Water Transportation	-3.2101	**	-3.0432	**	-2.2941	**
Air Transportation	-0.7102		-1.6359		0.1658	
Rail Transportation	0.4637		-0.0899		1.1566	
Trucks	-1.0539		-1.2724		0.0322	
Electricity	-5.4933	**	-5.2967	**	-2.9094	**
Gas	-4.1905	**	-2.4781	**	-3.3315	**
Petroleum Refining	-0.4474		0.6824		-1.3111	
Real Estate	-2.3702	**	-2.3062	**	-2.2973	**

Notes: 1. See chapter 2 for details of how these statistics are derived. 2. ** indicate significance at the 5% level.

Table 4.4.A also presents the average R^2 for each industry for the whole period and for the two subperiods. Since beta is a measure of market risk the average R^2 of each industry indicates how much of the total variation of that industry's returns can be attributed to market movements. Average R^2's range from 0.3526 (real estate industry) to 0.7127 (electricity industry) with the R^2 of the water transportation industry being relatively high at 0.6539. This implies that the variation in the returns of the water transportation industry are explained quite well by market movements in comparison to other industries such as real estate (0.3526).

Table 4.4.C: Testing the equality of betas between water transportation and other industries

Water Transportation beta versus beta of:	*1984:7-1995:6*		*1984:7-1989:12*		*1990:1-1995:6*	
	t-statistic		*t-statistic*		*t-statistic*	
Air Transportation	-0.8438		0.2397		-1.1871	
Rail Transportation	-1.9530	**	-0.7506		-2.4555	**
Trucks	-0.7378		0.2965		-1.6064	*
Electricity	-0.2596		0.9043		-0.7895	
Gas	-0.8124		-0.2002		-0.6811	
Petroleum Refining	-1.0410		-1.7803	**	-0.1631	
Real Estate	1.8964	**	1.8462	**	1.8503	**

Notes: 1. See chapter 2 for details of how these statistics are derived. 2. **, * indicate significance at the 5% and 10% level, respectively.

Another interesting observation emerging from table 4.4.A is that all average industry R^2's are increasing as we move from the first subperiod to the second. The R^2 of the water transportation industry is 0.6074 in the first subperiod while in the second it is 0.7115. This increasing trend of the R^2 means that market movements explain the variation of stock returns better in the second period than in the first.

Figure 4.4.A: Industry Average Returns and Betas for the period July 1984 - June 1995

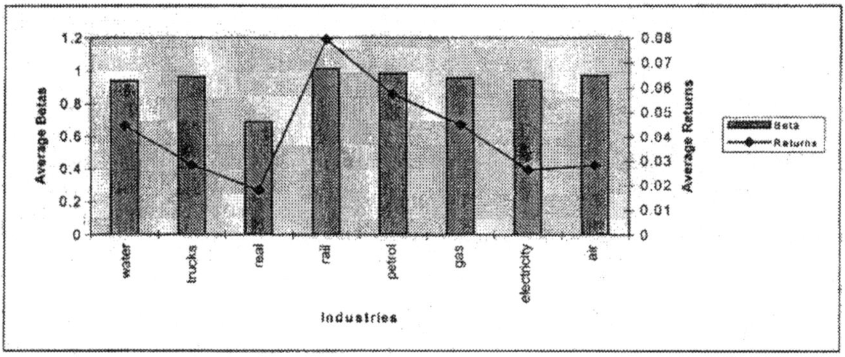

Figure 4.4.B: Industry Average Returns and Betas for the period July 1984 – Dec. 1989

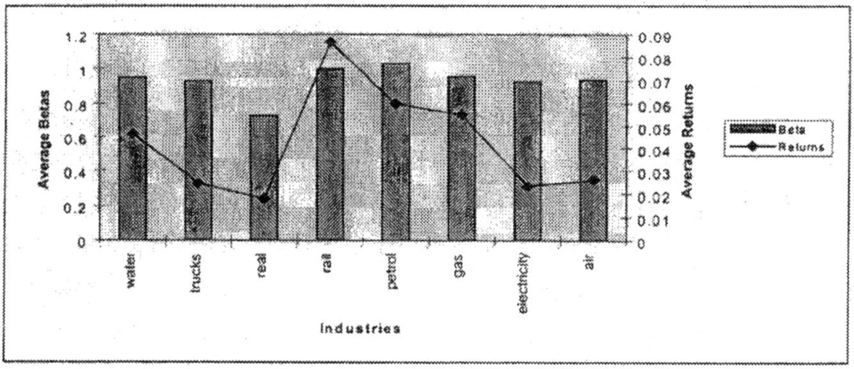

Figure 4.4.C: Industry Average Returns and Betas for the period January 1990 - July 1995

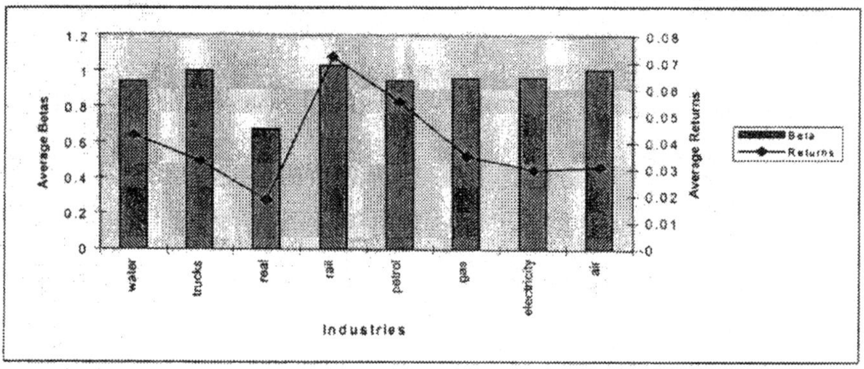

An important issue here is whether the systematic risk (as measured by beta) of the water transportation industry is different to that of other industries for the whole period and for the two subperiods. Results of this pairwise comparison of the average beta of the water transportation industry with the average beta of each of the other industries are in table 4.4.C.

For the full eleven-year period the average beta of the water transportation industry (0.9411) is significantly lower than that of the rail transportation industry (1.0155) and significantly higher than that of the real estate industry (0.6933). In the first subperiod it is (0.9472) significantly lower than that of the petroleum refining industry (1.0290) and significantly higher than that of the real estate industry (0.7242). Finally, in the second subperiod it is (0.9402) significantly lower than those of the rail transportation (1.0290) and trucks industry (1.0009) and significantly higher than that of the real estate industry (0.6705).

Having used the CAPM to model the returns of each of the eight industries and subsequently compare their systematic risks, the average of each industry is plotted against the corresponding average industry beta. Figures 4.4.A to 4.4.C depict this relationship for the full 11-year period and the two 66 month subperiods. As can be seen the industry with the higher average beta (rail transportation) exhibits the higher average returns while the industry with the lower beta (real estate) exhibits the lower returns. Although the water transportation industry's systematic risk is at similar or lower levels than those of the trucks, gas, electricity and air transportation industries, its average returns are higher than those of these industries are.

4.5. Conclusion

The results presented in this chapter indicate a number of interesting aspects of the behaviour of water transportation company stock returns from 1985 to 1995. Firstly, in both the tests carried out in sections 4.3 and 4.4 the average beta of companies in this sector were not found to be significantly higher than the beta of the "average" company which is unity. Moreover, in the tests carried out in section 4.4, the beta of the water transportation industry was found, along with the betas of the real estate, gas and electricity industries, to be significantly lower than that of the "average" company in the market. In contrast, the average betas of the air and rail transportation, trucks and petroleum refining industries were found to be equal to the market beta of unity. This result of the systematic - nondiversifiable risk of the water transportation industry being equal, if not smaller, than the average risk in the market could make the shipping industry attractive for potential investors.

Secondly, as was outlined in section 4.3, the systematic risk, as measured by beta, of water transportation companies has not changed over bull and bear market conditions during the 10 year period analysed. As a consequence, investors need not worry about changes in the systematic risk of their water transportation stocks over changing market conditions.

The third finding of this chapter, documented in section 4.3, is that there is a size effect in the shipping industry for the period 1984-1989. When the sample is partitioned by market value of equity it is found that smaller companies exhibited higher returns. However, as expected, these higher returns were found to be accompanied by higher total and higher systematic risk. The size effect, accompanied by a shift of small and medium companies towards large, disappears in the second period of our study. This finding is in line with other empirical evidence in the general finance literature.

Finally, as outlined in section 4.4, the average beta of the water transportation industry is significantly lower than that of the rail transportation industry for the whole period and for the second subperiod. It is also significantly lower than that of the petroleum refining industry for the first subperiod, while it is significantly higher than that of the real estate industry. It is insignificantly different to the beta of the other industries however.

CHAPTER 5: MICROECONOMIC (COMPANY SPECIFIC) FACTORS AS DETERMINANTS OF EQUITY RETURNS

5.1. Introduction

In this chapter, in addition to the market effect on equity returns, which was examined in some detail in chapter 4, the following set of microeconomic (accounting or company specific) factors are considered as possible determinants of stock returns: market value of equity, book-to-market value of equity ratio, earnings-to-price ratio, asset-to-market value of equity ratio, and asset-to-book value of equity ratio. As might be recalled from chapter 1, this set of factors has been investigated in the general literature on stock returns in the past. The findings of this chapter indicate that there are factors beyond the market which influence each industry's stock returns. These factors differ according to the industry being investigated.

Uncovering factors, other than the market, that may influence returns in the industries examined would enhance investment decisions and perhaps induce investors to place a different share of their investment funds in these industries. Also, if one assumes that the market value of stocks in these industries reflect correctly the economic fundamentals prevailing in each industry (as evaluated by the experts dealing in these shares), and also that the companies listed in the stock exchange are representative of their industries, then conclusions may be drawn regarding the opportunity costs and prospects of investing in each of these economic sectors for business.

5.2. A Possible Set of Relevant Macroeconomic Factors

A number of developments in the literature over the past years regarding determinants of stock returns point to using multifactor models, under which expected stock returns are influenced by additional factors other than the market risk. Fama and French (1992) examining portfolio classification of stocks use a set of microeconomic factors as determinants of the cross-section of expected stock returns in the US. The selection of such fundamental factors has been guided more by intuition and by their popularity among investment managers and academics than by any explicit theoretical model. As Fama (1991) points out, any correlation found between fundamental factors (micro or macro) and returns could be consistent with the factors proxying for omitted risk influences. If this correlation of returns to fundamental factors can be documented it may lead to a better understanding of the behaviour of stock prices, which in turn will result in better investment decisions.

The factors identified as significant by Fama and French (1992) are used in this chapter. In particular, apart from the significance of market risk, the significance of the following set of microeconomic factors, Market Equity (ME), Book to Market Equity ratio (BE/ME), Assets to Market Equity ratio (A/ME), Assets to Book Equity ratio (A/BE) and Earnings to Price ratio (E/P), are examined for companies in the water transportation sector and other transportation and non transportation sectors. Such an analysis would uncover the factors influencing returns in each industry, and these exposures to risk may be compared between sectors, resulting in more rational investment decisions.

In the US, the cross-sectional relationship between expected stock returns and fundamental factors has been studied extensively using cross-industry portfolios of companies. In general, a positive relationship has been found between stock returns and BE/ME, A/ME and E/P, and a negative relationship has been documented between stock returns and size (as measured by ME) and A/BE.

Thus, regarding the size effect Banz (1981), Basu (1977,1983), Reinganum (1981), Lakonishok and Shapiro (1986), Fama and French (1992) and others, find that the cross-section of average returns on small (low market equity) stocks are too high, whereas average returns on large stocks are too low. A possible explanation of this "size effect" is put forward by Roll (1981) who argues that small firms are not traded frequently and therefore their risk-return relationship is improperly measured[1]. In another explanation, Stoll and Whaley (1983) argue that transaction costs for small companies are larger than those for large companies therefore mitigating the associated excess returns.

Stattman (1980), Rosenberg, Reid, and Lanstein (1985) and Fama and French (1992) find that average returns on US stocks are positively related to BE/ME. A similar relationship is found for Japanese stocks by Chan, Hamao and Lakonishok (1991), who find that BE/ME has a strong role to play in explaining the cross-section of average stock returns, rather than size. Companies with high BE/ME ratios (low prices) are believed to be "value" stocks while companies with low BE/ME ratios (high prices) are believed to be "growth" stocks. Generally speaking, "growth" stocks are stocks having rapid increases in earnings, whereas "value" stocks are stocks whose market price seems to be low relative to their worth. The above empirical evidence therefore suggests that "value" stocks seem to outperform "growth" stocks.

Fama and French (1992), among others (e.g. Bhandari, 1988), also studied the effect of market leverage (A/ME) and book leverage (A/BE) on stock returns. They find that market leverage affects returns positively on average while book leverage affects returns negatively on average. Finally, Ball (1978), Reinganum (1981) and Basu (1983) argue that E/P ratios help explain the cross-section of average returns on US stocks by proxying for omitted risk factors.

5.3. Results – Identified Factors in each Industry

This section then, examines stock returns of eight industries using the stock market returns and the set of microeconomic factors mentioned above as explanatory variables. Based on past evidence of the studies listed earlier, stock returns vary directly with stock market returns (since the stock market conditions influence all stocks), the earnings to price ratio

[1] However, Reinganum (1982) estimated Dimson betas to overcome this problem, but he found that the use of these Dimson - adjusted estimates do not significantly alter the magnitude of the "size effect".

(since it may be taken as a proxy for omitted risk variables), the book to market ratio (since "value" stocks tend to outperform "growth" stocks), and the asset to market ratio (since higher stock returns are associated with high market leverage). Furthermore, stock returns vary inversely with the market value of equity (since small companies outperform large companies) and the asset-to-book ratio (since higher stock returns are associated with low book leverage).

Equation (5.1) is a compact mathematically expressed summary of the empirical (time-series) relation between stock returns, the stock market returns, and fundamental variables.

$$XR_{ijt} = f\,(XR_{Mt}, (E/P)_{ijt-6}, (ME)_{ijt-1}, (BE/ME)_{ijt-6}, (A/ME)_{ijt-6}, (A/BE)_{ijt-6}) + \varepsilon_{ijt} \quad (5.1)$$

where j is the company in industry i, t=1984:7,...,1995:6, XR_{ijt} are company j excess returns, XR_{Mt} are market excess returns, $(ME)_{ijt-1}$ are market values of equity lagged once, $(E/P)_{ijt-6}$, $(BE/ME)_{ijt-6}$, $(A/ME)_{ijt-6}$ and $(A/BE)_{ijt-6}$ are earnings to price ratios, book to market, asset to market and asset to book ratios, respectively, lagged 6 periods, and ε_{ijt} are white noise error terms. Logarithms of microeconomic variables are used during estimation. The estimated constant in the above equation indicates whether stock j of industry i is underpriced (when it is positive) or overpriced (when it is negative).

The fundamental variables in equation (5.1) are lagged as in Fama and French (1992). While a company's stock price changes every month, its accounting numbers are updated only once a year, in the month of announcement of the financial statements. However, all the fundamental variables except the asset-to-book ratio change every month because of the fluctuation in stock prices entering their definition. To ensure that the accounting variables are known before the returns they are used to explain, we match the accounting data for all fiscal yearends in calendar year[2] *TY-1* with the returns for July of year *TY* to June of *TY+1*. The 6-month gap between fiscal year end and the return tests are conservative and ensure that out tests are predictive in nature. Earlier studies (e.g. Basu, 1983) often assume that

[2] Note: TY refers to years while t refers to months.

accounting data are available within three months of fiscal yearends. Companies in the US are indeed required to file their 10-K reports with the SEC (Securities Exchange Commission) within 90 days of their fiscal yearends, but on average about 20% do not comply (Fama and French, 1992).

Equation (5.1) is estimated using SURE methods[3] and implies estimating the equation as a system of j stocks in each industry i, and allowing for cross-equation correlation in the residuals. As already mentioned in chapter 2, there are two advantages in such an approach: (1) betas are estimated simultaneously across companies with the impact of the fundamental variables, the alphas, thus allowing imposition of cross-equation restrictions on the parameters, and (2) the SURE procedure by adjusting for cross-equation correlation in the residual returns across companies leads to estimates which are more efficient than OLS; the gain being proportional to the degree of correlation between disturbances from the different equations. This second advantage is particularly important in this case since the companies are grouped according to their industry classification and thus their residual returns are likely to be correlated.

As in chapter 4, temporal analysis is undertaken by subdividing the 11-year period into two subperiods: July 1984 - December 1989, and January 1990 - June 1995. Such analysis enables us to observe whether betas and the fundamental microeconomic factors change through time for each industry.

The general-to-specific modelling procedure is used to select the "best" model for each industry. This involves estimating equation (5.1) by SURE for each industry and end-up with the model which includes only the significant variables. Past research (e.g. Chan, Hamao and Lakonishok, 1991, Fama and French, 1992) has presented models with each of the factors entering the model alone and also in combinations of the factors. Such procedure may lead to results which are subject to omitted variables bias (see for e.g. Pindyck and

---

[3] See among others Brown, Kleidon, and Marsh (1983), Jaffe, Keim, and Westerfield (1989) and Chan, Hamao and Lakonishok (1991) for applications of the SURE methodology in similar contexts.

Rubinfeld, 1991). Therefore, first we estimate the full model (equation (5.1)) and then, based on the set of significant factors obtained for each industry, estimate the version of equation (5.1), which includes only the set of significant factors. These versions of the full model are our final models for each industry for the eleven-year period (July 1984 - June 1995). They are presented in table 5.1 along with the one-factor, CAPM estimated parameters. Tables 5.2.A and 5.2.B present the corresponding models for each industry during the first (1984:7-1989:12) and second (1990:1-1995:6) subperiods analysed.

Market betas are positive and statistically significant for every company in every industry according to our a priori expectations. Their average values range from 0.689 (real estate industry) to 1.011 (rail transportation) for the whole period, 0.694 (real estate) to 1.016 (petroleum refining) for the first subperiod, and 0.701 (real estate) to 1.027 (rail transportation) for the second subperiod. The average market beta of the water transportation industry is 0.941 and is the lowest when compared to the betas of the other transportation sectors which are 0.976 for the air transportation industry, 1.011 for the rail transportation industry and 0.968 for the trucks industry, for the full eleven year period. Furthermore, only the real estate industry exhibits an average market beta which is lower than the average market beta of the water transportation industry. This implies that the water transportation industry exhibits the second lowest systematic (market) risk of the industries analysed.

The conclusions regarding the systematic risk of each industry remain unchanged when considered in the one factor CAPM context. However, the magnitude of the constant for each industry seems to change at least in some industries as we move from the single factor CAPM to the multifactor model. For example, the CAPM tends to overestimate the constant when compared to the multifactor model for six out of eight industries in our sample for the whole period. Therefore, the inclusion of the microeconomic factors tends to take away some of the underpricing suggested by the CAPM.

Table 5.1: Estimated Regressions of $XR_i = f(\overset{+}{XR_M}, \overset{+}{E/P}, \overset{-}{ME}, \overset{+}{BE/ME}, \overset{+}{A/ME}, \overset{-}{A/BE})$, for each Industry for the period July 1984 - June 1995

	Multifactor Model Estimates							CAPM Estimates	
INDUSTRY	**INTRCPT**	**XR_M**	**E/P**	**ME**	**BE/ME**	**A/ME**	**A/BE**	**INTRCPT**	**XR_M**
Air Transportation	0.003 *** (0.000)	0.976 *** (0.034)					-0.017 (0.006) ***	0.012 *** (0.003)	0.975 *** (0.036)
Rail Transportation	0.008 ** (0.004)	1.011 *** (0.032)				0.011 (0.005) ***		0.015 *** (0.003)	1.016 *** (0.033)
Trucks	0.021 *** (0.002)	0.968 *** (0.031)						0.021 *** (0.002)	0.968 *** (0.031)
Water Transportation	0.042 (0.000) ***	0.941 *** (0.019)					-0.007 (0.001) ***	0.035 *** (0.002)	0.941 *** (0.017)
Electricity	0.077 *** (0.002)	0.942 *** (0.010)			0.033 *** (0.002)			0.067 *** (0.002)	0.947 *** (0.010)
Gas	0.065 *** (0.004)	0.952 *** (0.010)		-0.004 *** (0.000)				0.045 *** (0.002)	0.958 *** (0.009)
Petroleum Refining	0.023 *** (0.008)	0.976 *** (0.038)		0.002 ** (0.001)		0.041 (0.004) ***	-0.015 (0.003) ***	0.034 *** (0.002)	0.984 *** (0.036)
Real Estate	0.028 *** (0.004)	0.689 *** (0.133)			0.034 *** (0.003)			0.026 *** (0.003)	0.693 *** (0.129)

Notes: 1. Numbers in parentheses are standard errors. 2. ***, ** and * indicate significance at 1%, 5% and 10% levels, respectively.

Table 5.2.A: Estimated Regressions of $XR_i = f(\overset{+}{XR_M}, \overset{+}{E/P}, \overset{-}{ME}, \overset{+}{BE/ME}, \overset{+}{A/ME}, \overset{-}{A/BE})$ for each Industry for the period July 1984 - December 1989

	Multifactor Model Estimates							CAPM Estimates	
INDUSTRY	**INTRCPT**	**XR_M**	**E/P**	**ME**	**BE/ME**	**A/ME**	**A/BE**	**INTRCPT**	**XR_M**
Air Transportation	0.014 *** (0.004)	0.937 *** (0.038)						0.014 *** (0.004)	0.937 *** (0.038)
Rail Transportation	0.006 (0.005)	0.994 *** (0.058)				0.014 (0.006) **		0.017 *** (0.003)	0.995 *** (0.061)
Trucks	0.017 *** (0.002)	0.930 *** (0.055)						0.017 *** (0.002)	0.930 *** (0.055)
Water Transportation	0.037 *** (0.003)	0.947 *** (0.017)						0.037 *** (0.003)	0.947 *** (0.017)
Electricity	0.085 *** (0.004)	0.925 *** (0.016)		-0.001 *** (0.000)	0.029 *** (0.002)			0.075 *** (0.003)	0.927 *** (0.014)
Gas	0.064 *** (0.005)	0.952 *** (0.020)		-0.003 *** (0.001)	0.011 *** (0.003)			0.051 *** (0.003)	0.953 *** (0.019)
Petroleum Refining	0.032 * (0.017)	0.997 *** (0.038)				0.068 (0.005) ***	-0.044 (0.006) ***	0.041 *** (0.004)	1.029 *** (0.043)
Real Estate	0.026 *** (0.005)	0.719 *** (0.124)			0.035 *** (0.009)			0.023 ** (0.005)	0.724 *** (0.130)

Notes: 1. Numbers in parentheses are standard errors. 2. ***, ** and * indicate significance at 1%, 5% and 10% levels, respectively.

Table 5.2.B: Estimated Regressions of $XR_i = f(\overset{+}{XR_M}, \overset{+}{E/P}, \overset{-}{ME}, \overset{+}{BE/ME}, \overset{+}{A/ME}, \overset{-}{A/BE})$ for each Industry for the period January 1990 - June 1995

	Multifactor Model Estimates							CAPM Estimates	
INDUSTRY	INTRCPT	XR_M	E/P	ME	BE/ME	A/ME	A/BE	INTRCPT	XR_M
Air Transportation	0.021 ***	1.010 ***					-0.014 **	0.009 ***	1.009 ***
	(0.008)	(0.049)					(0.007)	(0.003)	(0.051)
Rail Transportation	0.016 ***	1.029 ***						0.016 ***	1.029 ***
	(0.004)	(0.025)						(0.004)	(0.025)
Trucks	0.031 ***	0.994 ***			0.129 ***			0.020 ***	1.001 ***
	(0.000)	(0.027)			(0.004)			(0.002)	(0.027)
Water Transportation	0.037 ***	0.939 ***					-0.006 ***	0.030 ***	0.940 ***
	(0.000)	(0.027)					(0.002)	(0.002)	(0.026)
Electricity	0.072 ***	0.957 ***			0.032 ***			0.060 ***	0.963 ***
	(0.002)	(0.089)			(0.002)			(0.002)	(0.013)
Gas	0.057 ***	0.952 ***		-0.002 ***				0.043 ***	0.960 ***
	(0.005)	(0.012)		(0.001)				(0.002)	(0.012)
Petroleum Refining	-0.002	0.938 ***		0.005 ***		0.013 ***		0.028 ***	0.948 ***
	(0.007)	(0.040)		(0.001)		(0.001)		(0.003)	(0.004)
Real Estate	0.029 ***	0.666 ***			0.033 ***			0.027 ***	0.671 ***
	(0.004)	(0.147)			(0.007)			(0.004)	(0.143)

Notes: 1. Numbers in parentheses are standard errors. 2. ***, ** and * indicate significance at 1%, 5% and 10% levels, respectively.

The sensitivities of each industry's returns to the set of microeconomic factors are not uniform but their influence varies across industries and over time. In particular, there is a "size effect" in the gas and petroleum refining industries for the whole period. In the gas industry, as in the majority of the literature (e.g. Banz, 1981, Fama and French, 1992), higher returns are associated with "small" firms while lower returns are associated with "big" firms. This size effect is more pronounced in the first subperiod. In the petroleum refining industry however, in contrast to our a priori expectations, higher returns are associated with "big" firms and lower returns are associated with "small" firms. This positive "size" effect appears in the second subperiod. Finally, there is evidence of a negative "size" effect in the electricity industry, which is however evident only during the first subperiod studied.

The book-to-market equity ratio seems to have explanatory power over the cross-sectional returns of two industries, electricity and real estate, for the full eleven-year period. It has the expected positive sign (as in Fama and French, 1992), which implies that "value" stocks outperformed "growth" stocks in these two industries. This positive book-to-market effect is evident in both subperiods for both industries. Furthermore, there is a positive book-to-market effect in the gas industry for the first subperiod.

The measure of market leverage (asset-to-market equity ratio) seems to explain the cross-sectional returns of the rail transportation and petroleum refining industries over the whole eleven-year period. Its sign is positive as expected (e.g. Fama and French, 1992). This effect persists for both subperiods for the petroleum refining industry but is evident only in the first subperiod for the rail transportation industry.

The other measure of leverage, asset-to-book equity ratio (book leverage) is negatively related to the returns of three industries (as in Fama and French, 1992) for the full eleven year period; that is, for air transportation, water transportation and petroleum refining. This effect is concentrated in the first subperiod for the petroleum refining industry and in the second subperiod for the air and water transportation industries. It is worth noting here that the book leverage effect in the water transportation industry is much less than in the other two industries as can be seen from the corresponding coefficients.

The application of equation (5.1) in each industry has revealed that for seven out of eight industries analysed the market is not the only significant factor in explaining industry stock returns for the full eleven year time period. Other factors such as the market value of equity, the asset-to-book ratio, the asset-to-market ratio and the book-to-market ratio come out statistically significant quite often. The earnings-to-price ratio seems to play no role in explaining the returns of the companies belonging to the industries in our sample since it has not come out significant in any of the industries.

Temporal analysis has also revealed that in some cases (e.g. water and air transportation) the effect of the fundamental microeconomic factors is concentrated in only one subperiod. In other cases (e.g. real estate) there is a consistent pattern in the behaviour of these factors over time. Furthermore, there are cases where the significance and effect of the fundamental variables as measured by the magnitude of their coefficient varies from subperiod to subperiod (e.g. A/ME ratio in the petroleum refining industry).

Generally speaking the fundamental factors come out, at least in the majority of the industries, with the expected sign (consistent with the empirical evidence we have seen in the literature discussed earlier on in the chapter) both for the overall period and the two subperiods. The book leverage measure, A/BE, seems to affect negatively the returns of three industries, petroleum refining, air transportation and water transportation. The market leverage measure, A/ME, affects positively the returns of two industries petroleum refining and rail transportation. The book to market equity, BE/ME, is significant and positive in two industries, electricity, and real estate. Finally, there is a "size effect" in the gas (-ve), and the petroleum refining (+ve) industries.

5.4. Conclusion

The aim of this chapter has been to compare the riskiness of the water transportation industry to that of other transportation sectors and other related industries using a set of microeconomic factors as explanatory variables of returns. An augmented CAPM model with the following set of fundamental microeconomic factors, (1) Market Value of Equity, (2) Earnings to Price ratio, (3) Book to Market equity, (4) Asset to Book equity, (5) Asset to Market equity, proposed by a number of authors in the literature, has been employed during the estimation process. The SURE methodology was used for estimation purposes due to the advantage of adjusting the cross-sectional correlations among residual returns. This leads to more efficient estimates of the parameters of interest. Temporal analysis was also undertaken by dividing the eleven-year period into two equal subperiods.

Results indicate that there are factors other than the market that influence the returns of the water transportation industry and the other industries. The market seems to be the driving force behind returns in all industries. The significance of the other factors varies across sectors and over time. Book to market, asset to market and asset to book ratios, and the market value of equity become significant in some industries but not in others. The earnings to price ratio has no role to play in any industry. Generally speaking, the coefficients of the fundamental variables come out with the expected sign, with the exception of the positive "size effect" in the petroleum industry.

The water transportation industry, along with three other non-transportation industries exhibits lower than average systematic risk for the whole period studied as well as for the two subperiods. Only the real estate industry exhibits a lower beta than the water transportation industry over both subperiods. Based on the estimated numerical betas of the transportation sectors their ranking in ascending order is: Water (0.941), Trucks (0.968), Air (0.976) and Rail (1.011). The ranking is preserved in the second - most recent - subperiod.

To conclude then, under the axiom that industry returns unequivocally reflect changes in the risk of sectors, that is to say, that there is no gap between market perceptions about risk and reality, any differences in the perceived riskiness of the industries analysed in this book may have implications in an investment allocation process which allocates portions of a portfolio to several industries.

The findings of this chapter indicate that industry stock returns are linked, in addition to the market, to other microeconomic fundamental factors. It is not claimed, of course, that the set of fundamental factors employed in this chapter is exhaustive. However, we believe that by examining the sensitivities of industry stock returns to the set of fundamental microeconomic factors discussed in this chapter the investment manager may understand the behaviour of stock prices better and therefore make more informed investment decisions.

CHAPTER 6: MACROECONOMIC (ECONOMY WIDE) FACTORS AS DETERMINANTS OF EQUITY RETURNS

6.1. Introduction

This chapter builds upon the findings of chapter 5, which focused on the microeconomic factors affecting stock returns, and attempts to uncover the macroeconomic factors affecting stock returns of the industries analysed in this book. The use of risk measures derived from the market and the economy are appropriate for comparing risk profiles between industries under the assumption that markets are reasonably efficient. However, although a very interesting issue, the number of studies comparing risk across industries, in a macroeconomic context is limited both in number and in scope.

Isimbabi (1994) and Saunders and Yourougou (1990) for example are notable exceptions, which undertake a comparative analysis of the stock market perception of the risk of banks in comparison to other sectors such as utilities, petroleum refining, transportation et al. over time. Both studies are carried out in a multifactor model context to examine the sensitivity of the returns of companies in each industry grouping to a set of macroeconomic and industry risk factors.

To the best of our knowledge no study exists which compares the sensitivities to macroeconomic factors of the stock returns of transportation companies with those of non-- transportation sectors. Past studies in the US and elsewhere have examined the pricing of risk in relation to a set of macroeconomic factors by constructing portfolios of firms according to either size (e.g. Chen, Roll and Ross, 1986, Poon and Taylor, 1991) and lately according to industry classification (e.g. Chen and Jordan, 1993).

This chapter attempts to address this issue by undertaking a comparative analysis of companies belonging to the water transportation sector and companies in other transportation and non - transportation sectors not only in terms of market risk but also in terms of the following set of macro - economic factors identified in the earlier studies of Chen, Roll and Ross (1986), Poon and Taylor (1991) and Chen and Jordan (1993):

industrial production, inflation, the term structure of interest rates, consumption, and oil prices.

6.2. A Possible Set of Relevant Macroeconomic Factors

The selection of the relevant factors mentioned in section 6.1 has been guided both by past empirical work as well as intuition. Chen, Roll and Ross (1986), for example, used the Fama and MacBeth (1973) methodology in US data to find that the monthly growth in industrial production is positively related to stock returns, while unexpected inflation and the term structure of interest rates affect stock returns negatively. They, furthermore, found that annual growth in industrial production, changes in expected inflation, consumption and oil prices do not have any explanatory power over stock returns.

Poon and Taylor (1991) applied the Chen, Roll and Ross (1986) exercise to UK data and argued that the macroeconomic factors claimed by Chen, Roll and Ross (1986) to influence US stock returns do not affect stock returns in the UK. Other research findings include Hamao (1988) who performed similar tests for Japanese stocks and found strong pricing evidence as suggested by Chen, Roll and Ross (1986), except for the case of Japanese monthly growth in industrial production. Martinez and Rubio (1989) use Spanish stocks and like Poon and Taylor (1991) find no significant pricing relationship between Spanish stock returns and macroeconomic variables.

Chen and Jordan (1993) grouping firms in industries according to their SIC classification use a set of macroeconomic factors close to those of Chen, Roll and Ross (1986) and find, in contrast to the latter, that the returns on the market index and the change in oil prices, alongside the change in expected inflation are possible sources of risk.

Intuitively, the effect of macroeconomic factors on stock returns is thought to be a consequence of the pricing of stocks, as the stream of discounted expected future cash flows from holding a security. According to Damodaran (1994), the general stock valuation model mentioned above can be represented by the following equation:

$$\text{Price of Security} = \sum_{t=1}^{t=\infty} \frac{DPS_t}{(1+r)^t} \tag{6.1}$$

where DPS_t denote expected dividends per share and r is the required rate of return on stocks.

Macroeconomic factors which affect either the expectations of future dividends or the discount rate will consequently influence stock returns. Therefore, the macroeconomic factors employed in the papers mentioned above and in this paper are likely to affect stock returns in the following way:

Inflation: Inflation impacts both the level of the required rate of return and the size of the future cash flows. Therefore, its final effect cannot be deduced with any accuracy since the cash flow received increases but the rate used to discount it also increases.

The Term Structure of Interest Rates: Differences between the rate on bonds with a long maturity and a short maturity affect the value of payments far in the future relative to near term payments. Therefore, assuming the above difference to be positive, short-term dividend payments are discounted at a lower discount rate leading to higher initial cash flows. However, since returns are calculated over time as the ratio of Price (t) over Price (t-1), the positive cash flow effect is likely to weaken over time. Moreover, expectations of higher long - term rates might drive investors away from the stock market and thus lead to a decrease in prices and hence returns. Therefore, again one cannot deduce an explicit a priori relationship between stock returns and this factor.

Industrial Production: Increases in industrial production are associated with healthier economic conditions, affecting expectations positively on the numerator of equation (6.1), leading in turn to higher prices. In contrast to this, it is also argued that assuming that industrial production increases continuously, it is very likely that the economy will come to a state of "overheating" and the result will be restrictive government policies or rising interest rates which will affect the denominator of equation (6.1) positively, hence the valuation negatively.

Oil Prices: Irrespective of whether oil is an input or an output in an industry, oil prices affect the numerator of equation (6.1). If it is an input and the relevant industrial sector's capability to pass the full oil price increase to the consumer is limited, then the numerator of equation 1 and consequently the sector's valuation is affected negatively. If it is an output then it is likely that the numerator of equation (6.1) and the related sector's stock returns will increase.

Consumption: Rising consumption levels are usually associated with healthy economic conditions which in turn are associated with higher dividends and hence higher stock valuations. On the other hand, as is the case with industrial production rising consumption may cause an undesired expansion of the economy which might in turn lead to restrictive government policies which are likely to affect the numerator of equation (6.1) negatively and the denominator positively thus leading to lower stock valuations.

The examples of past efforts to model the macroeconomic determinants of stock returns discussed above indicate that the pricing relationships obtained in each case are not consistent. Consider for example Chen, Roll and Ross (1986) and Poon and Taylor (1991) who examined similar sets of macroeconomic factors, only to arrive at strikingly different results. The former found the majority of the factors to be significant while the latter concluded that the majority of the factors were not significant. As might be clear, differences among pricing relationships across studies makes any theoretical foundation regarding a priori expectations difficult and somewhat subjective. Hence, an open mind is kept regarding which of the above factors influence returns in individual industries and in what way, and we let this question be answered empirically.

6.3. Results – Identified Factors in each Industry

This section then attempts to uncover differences in the sensitivities of the stock returns of eight industries using the returns of the stock market and the set of macroeconomic variables mentioned in section 6.2. According to the definition of efficient markets, Fama (1970, 1976), stock prices should fully reflect all available information at any point in time. Therefore, unanticipated changes in the above factors, so-called news, are the relevant explanatory variables to include in the empirical work. Examples of applications of this theory may be found in Poon and Taylor (1991), Wasserfallen (1989) and Hardouvelis (1988).

Equation 6.2 is a compact, mathematically expressed summary, of the relation between stock returns of industry i, market returns and the aforementioned set of macroeconomic factors.

$$XR_{ijt} = f\,(XR_{Mt}, UMIP_t, UI_t, UTS_t, UOG_t, UCG_t) + \varepsilon_{ijt} \qquad (6.2)$$

where j is the company in industry i, t=1984:7,...,1994:6, XR_{ijt} are company j excess returns, XR_{Mt} are market excess returns, $UMIP_t$ denote unanticipated changes in monthly industrial production, UI_t are unanticipated changes in monthly inflation, UTS_t are unanticipated changes in the term structure of interest rates, UOG_t are unanticipated changes in oil prices, UCG_t are unanticipated changes in consumption, ε_{ijt} is a white noise error term. Details of how time series for each of these variables are derived, as well as concerns regarding possible multicollinearity between explanatory variables, are discussed in the data chapter, number 3. The empirical version of equation 6.2 can include a constant, which is expected to be zero if there is no mispricing of stocks. When the intercept is positive, stocks are underpriced and visa versa.

System-wide methods are convenient for empirical estimation of equation 6.2 since common coefficients over explanatory variables (the macroeconomic factors) may be imposed during estimation, thus assuming the role of industry averages. Adjustment for cross equation correlation using SURE methods to increase the efficiency of the estimated coefficients is not necessary however, since SURE estimates are equivalent to OLS when explanatory variables are identical across all equations in the system (see chapter 2 for details). However, if there are cross equation constraints on the parameters, such as when imposing common coefficients on the macro-factors, multi-equation least squares (MLSQ) methods may be used to estimate the equations as a system.

Table 6.5: Estimated Regressions $XR_i = f(XR_M, UMIP, UI, UTS, UOG, UCG)$ for each industry: July 1984 - June 1994

PANEL A: Multifactor Model Estimates (Long run coefficients)

Industry	Water Transportation	Air Transportation	Rail Transportation	Trucks	Electricity	Gas	Petroleum Refining	Real Estate
INTRCPT	0.0346***	0.0103***	0.0289***	0.0176***	0.0642***	0.0426***	0.0320***	0.0348***
	(0.0020)	(0.0031)	(0.0017)	(0.0026)	(0.0027)	(0.0017)	(0.002)	(0.0045)
XR_M	0.9449***	0.9538***	0.9875***	0.9698***	0.9248***	0.9579***	0.9741***	0.7543***
	(0.0195)	(0.0290)	(0.0178)	(0.0259)	(0.0267)	(0.0174)	(0.0202)	(0.134)
UMIP	-0.5363*				-1.1222***			
	(0.3262)				(0.4669)			
UTS		0.1497*		0.1332**	-0.1732**		0.1088*	
		(0.0819)		(0.0701)	(0.0781)		(0.0607)	
UOG	0.0422**			-0.0554**		0.0312*	0.1623***	-0.0420**
	(0.0175)			(0.0240)		(0.0170)	(0.0187)	(0.0177)
UCG			-0.7265*			-1.3657***		
			(0.4045)			(0.4506)		
UI								

PANEL B: CAPM Estimates

Industry	Water Transportation	Air Transportation	Rail Transportation	Trucks	Electricity	Gas	Petroleum Refining	Real Estate
INTRCPT	0.0336***	0.0111***	0.0154***	0.0207***	0.0614***	0.0433***	0.0330***	0.0249***
	(0.0019)	(0.0027)	(0.0027)	(0.0019)	(0.0026)	(0.0018)	(0.0024)	(0.0038)
XR_M	0.9571***	0.9496***	1.0127***	0.9816***	0.9464***	0.9521***	1.000***	0.7801***
	(0.0192)	(0.0271)	(0.0267)	(0.0185)	(0.0260)	(0.0179)	(0.0241)	(0.0377)

Notes: 1. Numbers in parenthesis are standard errors, Note 2. ***, **, * indicate significance at the 1%, 5%, and 10% levels respectively.

As in Chapter 5, the general - to - specific modelling procedure is utilised to select the "best" model for each industry. This involves employing MLSQ to estimate equation 6.2 for each industry for the time period July 1985 to June 1995, and by eliminating the non- - significant coefficients end up with the model which includes only the variables with coefficients which exhibit statistical significance. Thus, the full model (equation 6.2) is estimated for the ten year period (July 1985 - June 1994) and then, based on the set of significant factors obtained for each industry, the version of equation 6.2 which includes only the set of significant factors is estimated. Table 6.5 presents the final results along with the results of the one-factor CAPM, which are shown for comparative purposes.

The intercepts are positive and statistically significant for all industries, thus suggesting that companies in these industries have been underpriced on average during the ten-year period studied. The smallest underpricing occurs in the air transportation and trucks industries while the largest occurs in the electricity industry. The water transportation industry clearly exhibits the highest underpricing among the transportation sectors.

The market betas (coefficient of XR_M) are positive and statistically significant for every industry in the sample studied. They range between 0.754 (real estate industry) and 0.988 (rail transportation).[1] The water transportation industry exhibits a market beta of 0.945, which is the lowest among the transportation sectors and the third lowest among all sectors analysed. The market betas of the trucks and rail transportation industries are 0.970 and 0.988 respectively.

Table 6.6 presents t - tests regarding (1) the statistical equality of betas of each industry to unity i.e. to the market beta, and (2) the comparison of the beta of the water transportation industry to the betas of the seven other industries analysed. Panel A of table 6.6 indicates that the market beta, or systematic risk, of the water transportation industry, along with that of the electricity, gas and real estate industries are significantly lower than the average market beta of unity. These results are identical to those documented in chapter 5 of this book.

[1] A thorough discussion regarding the comparison of market betas across the eight industries can be found in chapter 4.

Table 6.6: Inferences regarding the market beta of the Water Transportation Industry

PANEL A: Tests of Equality of the average Betas of each industry, I, to the market beta of unity

Industry	Market Beta	t - statistic	
Water Transportation	0.9449	-2.8256	***
Air Transportation	0.9538	-1.5931	
Rail Transportation	0.9875	-0.7022	
Trucks	0.9698	-1.1660	
Electricity	0.9248	-2.8165	***
Gas	0.9579	-2.4195	***
Petroleum Refining	0.9741	-1.2822	
Real Estate	0.7543	-1.8336	*

Note: 1. See chapter 2 for details of how these statistics are derived. 2. ***, **, * indicate significance at the 1%, 5% and 10% level of significance, respectively.

PANEL B: Pairwise tests of equality of the market beta of the Water Transportation Industry and each of the other industries

Water Transportation beta versus beta of	t - statistic
Air Transportation	-0.2547
Rail Transportation	-1.6135
Trucks	-0.7680
Electricity	0.6079
Gas	-0.4974
Petroleum Refining	-1.0400
Real Estate	1.4076

Notes: 1. See chapter 2 for details of how these statistics are derived. 2. ***, **, * indicate significance at the 1%, 5% and 10% level of significance, respectively.

Turning now to panel B of table 6.6 it can be seen that the market beta of the water transportation industry does not exhibit any statistically significant difference to the market betas of all the other industries utilised in this study. This appears to be in some contrast to the results of the preceding chapter which indicated that the market beta of the water transportation industry is significantly lower than that of the rail transportation industry and significantly higher than that of the real estate industry. These differences are possibly due to the different model specifications and sample periods of the two papers.

Market betas of each industry estimated using the one - factor CAPM tend to exhibit differences to those estimated using the multifactor model thus suggesting that the inclusion of macroeconomic factors in the equation remedies any omitted variable bias that may be present in the CAPM specification.

As one might expect, the sensitivities of each industry's returns to the set of macroeconomic factors vary across industries. Specifically, the unexpected monthly growth rate in industrial production (UMIP) coefficient is significantly negative in the case of the water transportation and electricity industries. The strongest negative effect, as reflected by the corresponding coefficient (-1.1222), appears in the electricity industry. The negative coefficients of this variable are rather surprising since increases in industrial production tend to be associated with healthier economic conditions thus higher stock returns. On the other hand, unexpected announcements regarding healthier economic conditions might lead analysts to forecast more restrictive governmental policies in the future, since such shocks might well be the cause of future money growth and subsequently inflation, which in turn might lead to higher interest rates which could depress stock prices. It appears that for the water transportation and electricity industries the latter effect dominated the former.

It is not surprising then that the empirical evidence to date is not conclusive regarding this variable. Poon and Taylor (1991) for example, find stock returns to be negatively related to changes in monthly growth rates in industrial production, while Chen Roll and Ross (1986) document a positive relationship. Furthermore, Chen and Jordan (1993) find no significant relationship between monthly industrial production and stock returns.

The coefficient of unanticipated changes in the term structure variable (UTS) is statistically significant in four industries. The stock returns of the air transportation, trucks and petroleum refining industries are positively related to this variable while the stock returns of the electricity industry are negatively related to it. This implies that larger unanticipated changes in spreads between short - term and long - term interest rates affect positively the stock performance of two transportation (air transportation, and trucks) and one non - transportation (petroleum refining) sector, while such spreads affect negatively the stock performance of one non - transportation (electricity) sector. The positive effect of unanticipated changes in the term structure appears to be stronger in the air transportation and trucks industries.

Results regarding unanticipated changes in the term structure are somewhat different to the literature. Chen, Roll and Ross (1986) document a negative, although only marginally significant, relationship between stock returns and the term structure of interest rates. However, it should be noted that they did not use the unanticipated but the original series for this variable. Poon and Taylor (1991) and Chen and Jordan (1993) used the unanticipated series and found it to be insignificant.

Unanticipated changes in oil prices (UOG) are statistically significant in five out of the eight industries analysed, with three of the significant coefficients positive (water transportation, gas and petroleum refining) and two negative (trucks and real estate). Therefore, here lies strong evidence that unexpected increases in oil prices affect the stock returns of the different industries in different ways. Its positive effect appears to be more profound in the water transportation and gas industries while its negative effect is more dominant in the case of the trucks industry.

The advantage of analysing stock returns by industry can be seen clearly here in that it enables estimation of separate effects of each factor in every industry according to the economic effect of the factor on the industry. For example, rising oil prices might imply stockbuilding by several governments or large companies, a fact that might imply increased demand for water transportation hence higher freight rates thus higher profits and subsequently better stock price performance. On the other hand, rising oil prices imply higher costs hence less profits and lower stock prices for air transportation and trucks companies.

The coefficient of the fifth explanatory variable, unanticipated changes in consumption (UCG), is statistically significant only for two industries, rail transportation and gas. Results imply that higher unanticipated consumption is accompanied by lower returns in the aforementioned industries. In the literature, Lucas (1978) and Breeden (1979) argue, from a theoretical point of view, that consumption pricing models should imply a positive relationship between consumption and asset prices. The results of this chapter do not appear to be in line with such pricing models but are nevertheless in line with the results of Wasserfallen (1989) regarding the relationship between the stock returns and consumption in Switzerland. Furthermore, when consumption was included in the multifactor model of Chen, Roll and Ross (1986), it also came out with a negative sign but it was insignificant.

The final macroeconomic factor employed, unanticipated inflation (UI), does not appear to affect the returns of any industry. This contrasts with the results of Chen, Roll and Ross (1986) and Wasserfallen (1989) who document a significant negative relationship between stock returns and inflation

In sum, the application of equation 6.2 in each of the eight industries has revealed that for all industries analysed, the market is not the only significant (priced) factor in explaining stock returns. Macroeconomic factors also come out as significant in explaining the stock returns of each industry. Furthermore, the estimation of Equation 6.2 for each industry sheds some light on the differences in the structure and sensitivities of each industry's stock returns to the macroeconomic factors employed. Here, in our opinion, lies the major usefulness of such analysis; for example, the stock returns of the water transportation industry are affected by a different set of factors when compared to the air transportation industry. Furthermore, the industry analyst can also compare the direction, through the sign of the coefficient, as well as the significance of the sensitivities of the different factors employed in the analysis to the returns of each industry according to the economic impact of the factor on the industry; for example an unanticipated change in oil prices affects the petroleum refining industry much more than the gas industry.

6.4. Conclusion

The aim of the sixth chapter of this book has been to compare the riskiness of the water transportation industry to that of other transportation sectors and other related industries using multifactor models with macroeconomic variables as explanatory factors. The traditional CAPM was therefore augmented to include the following set of fundamental macroeconomic factors: (1) industrial production, (2) the term structure of interest rates, (3) oil prices, (4) consumption, and (5) inflation. The unanticipated part of the above variables was utilised in accordance with the theory of efficient markets, which suggests that only "news" should affect stock returns.

The results of this exercise indicate that, as in the case of chapter 5, there are factors other than the market that influence the returns of the water transportation industry and other industries, thus justifying the use of multifactor models instead of the traditional CAPM. Nevertheless, as one might have expected, the market influences the returns of all industries. Regarding the fundamental macroeconomic factors, it was found that their effect varies across industries.

Thus, monthly changes in industrial production are negatively related to the stock returns of the water transportation and electricity industries. This result is rather surprising since rising levels of industrial production are associated with higher stock returns. The unanticipated changes in the term structure of interest rates influence the returns of four industries, air transportation, trucks, electricity and petroleum refining. It positively affects the returns of the air transportation, trucks and petroleum refining industries and negatively affects the returns of the electricity industry. Unanticipated changes in oil prices are positively related to the water transportation, gas, and petroleum refining industries while at the same time they are negatively related to the trucks and real estate industries. Unanticipated changes in consumption seem to be negatively related to the returns of the rail transportation and gas industries while the final macroeconomic factor used, unanticipated inflation, appears not to affect the stock returns of any industry.

To conclude then, probably the most interesting and important finding of this chapter is that different industries react differently to changes in macroeconomic factors. It is possible that other macroeconomic factors influence returns. As long as one recognises this and takes them into account better informed investment decisions can be made.

CHAPTER 7: MICROECONOMIC AND MACROECONOMIC FACTORS - A UNIFIED APPROACH

7.1. Introduction

Chapters 5 and 6 of this book utilised multiequation multifactor models whose explanatory variables have been, in the case of chapter 5, a set of microeconomic factors and in the case of chapter 6, a set of macroeconomic factors. The set of microeconomic factors utilised in chapter 5 was initiated in the seminal paper of Fama and French (1992) and others such as Banz (1981), Bhandari (1988), Chan, Hamao and Lakonishok (1991), Brown, Kleidon and Marsh (1983) and many others. These factors are the market value of equity; the earnings-to-price ratio; the asset-to-market value of equity; and the asset-to- book value of equity. Similarly, the set of macroeconomic factors utilised in chapter 6 was initiated in the study of Chen, Roll and Ross (1986) and further investigated in the papers of Ferson and Harvey (1991), Hardouvelis (1988), Martinez and Rubio (1989), Wasserfallen (1989) and Poon and Taylor (1991). The factors employed, other than the market, are unanticipated changes in the following set of macroeconomic factors: industrial production, the term structure of interest rates, oil prices, consumption, and inflation.

Given the evidence presented in chapters 5 and 6, this chapter recognises that both micro and macro economic factors may be determinants of stock returns, and attempts to uncover the determinants of industry stock returns in a more general setting, where both sets of factors are included. These determinants of stock returns are then compared across industries and hence conclusions are drawn regarding the risk-return relationship of each industry in a broader context, featuring both microeconomic and macroeconomic parameters.

7.2. A Possible Set of Relevant Micro and Macroeconomic Factors

The set of microeconomic and macroeconomic factors mentioned in section 7.1, used to examine cross-sectional differences in industry stock returns, is drawn upon chapters 5 and 6 and may also be found in Fama and French (1992) [microeconomic factors] and Chen, Roll and Ross (1986) [macroeconomic factors], amongst others. Equation (7.1) is a mathematically expressed summary of the empirical relationship between stock returns, stock market returns, microeconomic and macroeconomic variables.

$$XR_{ijt}=f\{XR_{Mt},E/P_{ijt-6},ME_{ijt-1},BE/ME_{ijt-6},A/ME_{ijt-6},A/BE_{ijt-6},UMIP_{it},UI_{it},UTS_{it},UOG_{it},UCG_{it})+\varepsilon_{ijt} \quad (7.1)$$

where j is the company in industry i, t=1984:7,...,1995:6, XR_{ijt} are company j excess returns, XR_{Mt} are market excess returns, $(ME)_{ijt-1}$ are market values of equity lagged once, $(E/P)_{ijt-6}$, $(BE/ME)_{ijt-6}$, $(A/ME)_{ijt-6}$ and $(A/BE)_{ijt-6}$ are earnings to price ratios, book to market, asset to market and asset to book ratios, respectively, lagged 6 periods. Logarithms of microeconomic variables are used during estimation. Also, the set of macroeconomic factors included are denoted $UMIP_{it}$ for unanticipated changes of monthly growth rates in industrial production, UI_{it} for unanticipated changes of monthly inflation, UTS_{it} for unanticipated changes of the term structure, UOG_{it} for unanticipated changes of monthly growth rates in oil prices, UCG_{it} for unanticipated changes of monthly growth rates in consumption, and ε_{ijt} a white noise error term. As in the cases of the previous chapters, the empirical specification of equation (7.1) also includes a constant, whose expected value is zero assuming that there is no mispricing of the stocks. When the constant is positive, stocks are underpriced and when it is negative they are overpriced.

As in the case of chapter 6 and assuming market efficiency, the macroeconomic factors entering equation (7.1) have been filtered in an attempt to separate expected and unexpected changes in these factors; see chapter 3 for details. Another issue, relating to the macroeconomic variables included in equation (7.1) is that correlations between them are relatively low, mediating any a priori expectations of possible multicollinearity that might have existed between the variables.

SURE methods are used for estimation of equation (7.1) as a system of j stocks in each industry i, allowing for cross-equation correlation in the residuals. The following two advantages of SURE over single equation methods lead us to this choice: (1) betas are estimated simultaneously across companies (within the same industry) with the impact of the microeconomic and macroeconomic variables, and (2) SURE estimates, by adjusting for the correlation in the residual returns across companies, are more efficient than those obtained by OLS; the gain being proportional to the correlation between disturbances from the different equations. This second advantage is particularly important in this study since our companies are grouped according to their industry classification and thus their residual returns are likely to be correlated.

7.3. Results – Identified Factors in each Industry

Along the lines discussed in chapters 5 and 6, the general - to - specific modelling procedure is utilised to select the "best" model for each industry for the period July 1985 to June 1995. This requires estimation of equation (7.1), during the aforementioned period, using the SURE methodology for each industry and by the process of elimination of non-significant coefficients, end up with the model, which includes only the significant variables. The final models for each industry for the ten-year period (July 1985 - June 1995) are presented in table 7.1 along with the one-factor, CAPM estimated parameters.

The intercepts (INTRCPT) are all numerically positive and statistically significant, which implies that all industries appear to be underpriced. The electricity and gas industries appear to be the ones with the highest underpricing while petroleum refining and air transportation have the lowest underpricing. The underpricing of the water transportation, trucks, real estate and rail transportation industries lies in the 2% - 4% boundary.

Table 7.1: Regressions of XRi = f(XRM, E/P, ME, BE/ME, A/ME, A/BE, UMIP, UI, UTS, UOG, UCG) for each industry

for the period July 1984 - June 1995

PANEL A: Multifactor Model Estimates

Industry	Water Transportation	Air Transportation	Rail Transportation	Trucks	Electricity	Gas	Petroleum Refining	Real Estate
INTRCPT	0.0334 *** (0.0109)	0.0206 *** (0.0053)	0.0289 *** (0.0018)	0.0228 *** (0.0034)	0.0710 *** (0.0028)	0.0603 *** (0.0042)	0.0197 *** (0.0076)	0.0348 (0.0045)
XRM	0.9438 *** (0.0198)	0.9471 *** (0.0530)	0.9879 *** (0.0330)	0.9593 *** (0.0258)	0.9264 *** (0.0112)	0.9580 *** (0.0121)	0.9676 *** (0.0338)	0.7543 (0.1340)
E/P								
ME	0.0037 ** (0.0015)					-0.0028 *** (0.0005)	0.0023 *** (0.0009)	
BE/ME					0.0256 *** (0.0020)			
A/ME							0.0327 *** (0.0036)	
A/BE	-0.0064 ** (0.0013)	-0.0153 *** (0.0061)					-0.0140 *** (0.0031)	
UMIP	-0.5846 * (0.3416)				-1.0421 *** (0.4650)			
UI								
UTS		0.1801 * (0.0953)		0.1330 * (0.0776)	-0.1645 ** (0.0778)		0.1025 * (0.0624)	
UOG	0.0406 *** (0.0176)	-0.0931 *** (0.0293)		-0.0556 *** (0.0239)		0.0341 ** (0.0168)	0.1662 *** (0.0192)	-0.0420 (0.0177)
UCG			-0.7265 * (0.4295)			-1.3295 *** (0.4450)		

PANEL B: CAPM Estimates

Industry	Water Transportation	Air Transportation	Rail Transportation	Trucks	Electricity	Gas	Petroleum Refining	Real Estate
INTRCPT	0.0336 *** (0.0019)	0.0111 *** (0.0027)	0.0154 *** (0.0027)	0.0207 *** (0.0019)	0.0614 *** (0.0026)	0.0433 *** (0.0018)	0.0330 *** (0.0024)	0.0249 (0.0038)
XRM	0.9550 *** (0.0195)	0.9496 *** (0.0271)	1.0127 *** (0.0267)	0.9816 *** (0.0185)	0.9464 *** (0.0260)	0.9521 *** (0.0179)	1,000 *** (0.0241)	0.7801 (0.0377)

Notes: 1. Numbers in parenthesis are standard errors, 2. ***, **, * indicate significance at the 1%, 5% and 10% level of significance respectively.

Market betas (the coefficient of XR_M) are positive and statistically significant for all industries in the sample examined and range between 0.7543 (real estate industry) to 0.9879 (rail transportation industry). The market beta of the water transportation industry stands at 0.9438 and appears to be the lowest in the transportation sector and the third lowest, ranking behind real estate and electricity, of all the industries analysed. Market betas estimated in a one - factor, CAPM context, tend to be overestimated when compared to the ones obtained in a multifactor model context, thus suggesting that the inclusion of micro and macro - economic factors in the equation might remedy omitted variables bias.

Table 7.2: Inferences regarding the market beta of the Water Transportation Industry

PANEL A: Tests of Equality of the Betas of each Industry and the market betas

Industry	*Market Beta*	*T-statistic*	
Water Transportation	0.9438	-2.8384	***
Air Transportation	0.9471	-0.9981	
Rail Transportation	0.9879	-0.3667	
Trucks	0.9593	-1.5775	
Electricity	0.9264	-6.5714	***
Gas	0.9580	-3.4711	***
Petroleum Refining	0.9676	-0.9586	
Real Estate	0.7543	-1.8336	*

Notes: 1. See chapter 2 for details of how these statistics are derived. 2. ***,**,* indicate significance at the 1%, 5% and 10% level of significance, respectively.

PANEL B: Tests of Equality of market betas between the Water Transportation and other Industries

Water Transportation beta versus beta of	**T - statistic**
Air Transportation	-0.0839
Rail Transportation	-1.1459
Trucks	-0.4766
Electricity	0.7649
Gas	-0.6119
Petroleum Refining	-0.6076
Real Estate	1.3990

Notes: 1. See chapter 2 for details of how these statistics are derived. 2. ***, **, * indicate significance at the 1%, 5% and 10% level of significance respectively.

Table 7.2 presents t - tests regarding (1) the statistical equality of betas of each industry to unity, i.e. the market beta, and (2) the comparison of the beta of the water transportation industry to the betas of the seven other industries analysed. Panel A of table 7.2 indicates that the market beta, or systematic risk, of the water transportation industry, along with that of the electricity, gas and real estate industries are significantly lower than the average market beta of unity. These results are identical to those documented in chapters 5 and 6.

Turning now to panel B of table 7.2 it can be seen that the market beta of the water transportation industry does not exhibit any statistically significant difference to the market betas of all the other industries utilised in this study. This appears to be in some contrast to the results documented in the two previous chapters, which indicate that the market beta of the water transportation industry is significantly lower than that of the rail transportation industry and significantly higher than that of the real estate industry. These differences are thought to be due to the different model specifications and time horizons of the two studies.

The sensitivities of each industry's returns to the set of macroeconomic and microeconomic factors, as expected, vary across industries. Specifically, The monthly unexpected growth rate in the industrial production (UMIP) coefficient is statistically significant in two of the eight industries analysed but with a negative sign. More specifically, the stock returns of the water transportation industry and the electricity industry are negatively related to monthly growth rates in industrial production. The corresponding coefficients are -0.5846 for the water transportation industry and -1.0421 for the electricity industry and might be considered to be somewhat surprising since increases in industrial production tend to be associated with healthier economic conditions and thus higher stock returns. Nevertheless, as has already been discussed in chapter 6, output surprises may, on some occasions, cause analysts and investors to forecast more restrictive policy in the future since such shocks might be the cause of future inflation. In this case, if investors perceive that the authorities will not accommodate such increases, interest rates may rise and stock prices may fall.

As in the case of chapter 6, the coefficient of unanticipated changes in the term structure variable (UTS) is statistically significant in four of the eight industries analysed; the air transportation industry, the trucks industry, the electricity industry, and the petroleum refining industry. There appears to be a positive relationship between unanticipated changes in the term structure and the air transportation, trucks and petroleum refining industries and a negative one between this variable and the electricity industry. This implies that larger unanticipated changes in the spreads between short - term and long - term interest rates affect positively the stock market performance of the air transportation, trucks and petroleum refining industries and negatively the performance of the electricity industry.

Unanticipated changes in oil prices (UOG) appear to be significant in six of the eight industries under analysis. They exhibit a positive relationship in the water transportation, gas and petroleum refining industries and a negative relationship in the air transportation, trucks and real estate industries. Results regarding this variable appear to be in line with those documented in chapter 6 (with the exception of the air transportation industry whose coefficient is marginally insignificant) and point to the direction that the majority of the industries analysed are indeed affected by rising oil prices, one way or another. The positive relationship appears to be stronger in the petroleum refining industry while the negative relationship appears to be stronger in the air transportation industry.

The next macroeconomic variable utilised in equation (7.1), unanticipated changes in consumption (UCG), appears to be negatively related to the returns of the rail transportation and gas industries. This is in line with the results of the previous chapter and contrasts the theory of consumption pricing models, which imply a positive relationship between consumption and asset prices. In line with the findings of chapter 6, the final macroeconomic variable utilised, unanticipated inflation (UI), does not appear to affect the stock returns of any of the industries analysed.

As in the case of the macroeconomic factors, the sensitivities of each industry's returns to the set of microeconomic factors varies across industries. Thus, there is a "size effect" in three out of the eight industries analysed. In the water transportation industry, in contrast to the majority of the available literature, there is a positive "size effect" implying that stocks of larger water transportation companies' perform better than those of smaller companies. A similar relationship, of smaller magnitude though, is obtained for the petroleum refining industry, while for the gas industry a negative "size effect" is documented. The evidence depicted here is in some contrast to that of chapter 5, which suggests that there is a positive "size effect" in the petroleum refining industry and a negative "size effect" in the gas industry. Nevertheless, in contrast to this chapter, it does not document any relationship between size and the water transportation industry.

The book-to-market equity ratio, as in the case of chapter 5, seems to have explanatory power over the returns of the electricity industry only, where it comes out with the expected positive sign (as in Fama and French, 1992). The above results regarding the book-to-market ratio imply that "value" stocks in the electricity industry tend to outperform "growth" stocks.

The asset-to-book equity ratio, a measure of book leverage is statistically significant in three industries, water transportation, air transportation, and petroleum refining. It comes out with the expected negative sign (as in Fama and French, 1992) in all three industries. As can be seen from table 7.1), the negative effect of book leverage is more profound in the case of the air transportation industry.

The other measure of leverage (market leverage), the asset-to-market ratio, is statistically significant in just one industry, petroleum refining. In line with the existing literature (Fama and French, 1992), the sign of the coefficient is positive, a fact which implies that the stock returns of the petroleum refining industry are positively related to higher levels of market leverage. The final micro-economic factor utilised in the analysis, the earnings-to-price ratio does not appear to be priced in any of the industries analysed.

In sum, the application of equation (7.1) in each of the eight industries has revealed that for all industries analysed the market is not the only significant (priced) factor in explaining stock returns. Macroeconomic and microeconomic factors also come out as significant in explaining the stock returns of each industry. Furthermore, the estimation of equation (7.1) for each industry sheds some light regarding differences in the structure and sensitivities of each industry's stock returns to the set of factors employed. For example, the stock returns of the water transportation industry are affected by a different set of factors when compared to the air transportation industry. Furthermore, the industry analyst can also compare the direction, through the sign of the coefficient, as well as the significance of the sensitivities of the different factors employed in the analysis to the returns of each industry according to the economic impact of the factor on the industry; for example an unanticipated change in oil prices affects the petroleum refining industry much more than the gas industry or the negative effect of book leverage is more profound in the air transportation industry than in the water transportation industry.

7.4. Conclusion

As was the case with the previous two chapters, the aim of this, the seventh chapter of the book, has been to compare the riskiness of the water transportation industry to that of other transportation sectors and other related industries using multifactor models. The difference between this and the proceeding two chapters is that the traditional CAPM was augmented to include both microeconomic and macroeconomic factors. The microeconomic factors employed are those utilised in chapter 5 (the market value of equity (size); the book-to-market value of equity ratio; the earnings-to-price ratio; the asset-to-market value of equity ratio; and the asset-to-book value of equity ratio), while the macroeconomic factors used are those utilised in chapter 6 (industrial production; the term structure of interest rates; oil prices; consumption; and inflation).

The results of this chapter indicate that, as in the case of chapters 5 and 6, there are factors other than the market that influence the returns of the water transportation industry and other industries, thus justifying the use of multifactor models instead of the traditional CAPM. Having said that, it should be noted that the market is highly significant in explaining the returns of all industries analysed.

The significance of the other factors, microeconomic and macroeconomic, varies in direction and magnitude across industries. All factors, except unanticipated inflation and the price to earnings ratio appear to be significant in one industry or another. Their sign however is not always in line with the existing literature thus pointing out that empirical results regarding the direction of the determinants of industry returns may differ, in some cases, to the direction of the determinants of the returns of the full universe of stocks. This is in our opinion an important result of this research and an area, which could provide interesting research possibilities for the industry analyst.

Chapter 8: Macroeconomic Factors and International Industry Returns

By

Manolis G. Kavussanos, Stelios N. Marcoulis and Angelos G. Arkoulis

8.1 Introduction

This chapter extends the evidence presented in earlier chapters of the book, with respect to macroeconomic factors affecting industry returns, by moving away from the US and into a global setting. Managers who are interested in building global portfolios of stocks operate in such a setting. Evidence at the industry level[1], has shown that firms within the same industry experience similar rates of return. Furthermore, industry average rates of return exhibit significant differences; and this is reflected in the increasing focus of investors towards an industry oriented approach by the existence of sector funds (e.g. transport, construction, banking etc.).

Most studies on industry returns and risk, though, have been performed across individual countries, as demonstrated in earlier chapters. However, it would be interesting to examine industry stock returns at the global level. At this level, past studies have focused on whether country effects are more important than industry effects[2] on stock returns, and on the current degree of global capital market integration[3]. Rouwenhorst (1999), in a recent study, finds that country effects in stock returns continue to dominate industry effects for the European Monetary Union member countries, despite their increasing degree of coordination in their fiscal and monetary policies following the Maastricht Treaty. Furthermore, Capaul (1999) examines several pricing anomalies in industry specific, instead of country specific, portfolios. Weiss (1998) argues that, as capital market integration develops, and certain global industries are to a certain degree homogeneous, the industrial classification of a given asset becomes increasingly important to the investor.

---

[1] e.g. King (1966), Nerlove (1968), Fabozzi and Francis (1979).
[2] e.g. Grinold et al (1989), Roll (1992).
[3] e.g. Campbell and Hamao (1989), Gultekin et al (1989).

Generally, the degree of integration in various industries is such, at the international level, that global asset management firms increasingly place an industry focus in their research. In addition, the world economy is becoming increasingly more globalised with companies operating across borders, forming alliances/mergers in several industrial sectors, in some of them more than others. Given this industry internationalisation in the world economy it would be of interest to investors to understand the factors affecting risk levels across companies at the international level. Any possible relationship between a set of prespecified global risk factors and fluctuations in international industry stock returns can be beneficial to the investor in the sense that he can increase his diversification capacity or even speculate by timing his investment.

Thus, the objective of this chapter is to present evidence about the ability and the usefulness of world macroeconomic news in explaining the variability of global industry returns.[4] To the best of our knowledge, no study has performed this task.

Availability of global industry returns for 38 international industries, as compiled by Morgan Stanley Capital International (MSCI), makes such an analysis feasible. MSCI compile this unique database of global industry indices which replicates the industrial composition of each local market and forms each industry index from a total of approximately 1600 securities in 22 countries. The MSCI indices are value-weighted and aim for 60% coverage of the total market capitalisation.

This study focuses on the impact of a set of prespecified global risk variables on international industry returns, through time. These monthly risk variables are: the returns on a world equity market portfolio, fluctuations in global exchange rates, oil prices, global measures of inflation, industrial production growth and credit risk. Berry et al (1988), and additional evidence presented in earlier chapters of this book, suggest that the macro-economy has different effects across several industries. This makes a-priori expectations difficult to determine. The effect of a global risk factor could be positive in a particular industry and negative or insignificant in another, depending on the specific characteristics of each industry.

---

[4] The average return premia associated with industry returns are beyond the scope of this chapter.

This chapter is organised into five sections. The next section describes the macroeconomic variables included in the study. Section 3 describes the data and the derivation of the global risk factors, together with the methodological aspects of the approach employed to empirically test for the impacts of these factors on international industry returns. Results are reported in section 4, while section 5 summarises the findings and offers some concluding remarks.

8.2 Methodology

Although empirical studies on modelling the macroeconomic determinants of stock returns have focused on a similar set of variables, the significant relationships obtained in each case differ. These findings make any a priori expectations difficult to determine and to a certain degree subjective. It is then a matter of empirical evidence to determine whether and to what extent global returns on individual industries react to changes in global macroeconomic conditions.

In an efficient market, prices should reflect all available information at any point in time. Thus, as has been suggested by Chan et al (1985), Bernard (1986), Wasserfallen (1989), Poon and Taylor (1991) amongst others, innovations in macroeconomic factors are the relevant explanatory variables of the risk premia awarded in the stock market. Therefore, ARIMA models are used to filter out the expected component of each macroeconomic variable, and the 'news' components are used as explanatory variables of international industry returns.

The aim of this study is to uncover differences in the impacts on the returns of 38 international industries, using the returns of the world market portfolio and innovations in the following pre-specified set of global macroeconomic factors: a) exchange rates, b) changes in oil prices, c) global inflation, d) industrial production growth and e) credit risk. Equation (8.1) expresses this mathematically:

$$XR_{it} = f\,(WDRET_t,\ UdG10FX_t,\ UTLP_t,\ UdTED_t,\ UdOIL_t,\ UdG7IP_t) + \varepsilon_{i,t} \quad (8.1)$$

where $XR_{i,t}$ WDRET, UdG10FX, UTLP, UdTED, UdOIL, UdG7IP and ε_{it} are excess returns in industry i, the excess return on the world equity market, unexpected changes in global exchange rates against the dollar, unexpected global inflation, the unexpected component of global credit risk, unexpected changes in oil prices, unexpected changes in global monthly industrial production and the regression error term, respectively.

These macroeconomic factors stem from the work of Chen et al (1986) and Ferson and Harvey (1994). The former study was the first to suggest several observable factors, whereas the latter has employed a similar set of factors in an international context.

The excess return on the world equity market, WDRET, is included as a proxy for the 'world market' portfolio. Harvey (1991) finds that the MSCI world equity index has considerable explanatory power in the set of 22 MSCI country returns. It is therefore of interest to further examine the ability of the MSCI world equity index to explain the variability of industry returns at the global level.

Several empirical studies investigate and establish a relationship between foreign exchange risk, dG10FX, and equity returns. The findings of Dumas and Solnik (1995), for instance, justify the existence of time-varying foreign exchange risk premia in the international financial markets. Ferson and Harvey (1994), using a similar aggregate measure of exchange risk as in this paper, find that the variable is priced across 18 national equity markets.

Unexpected global inflation, UTLP, is another potential worldwide source of risk. Chen et al (1986), Ferson and Harvey (1994) and Chen and Jordan (1993) include an unanticipated inflation variable in their studies following the economic intuition that inflation, be it expected or unexpected, influences expected cash flows and thus returns[5]. Inflation, however, is also included in our study, because asset returns can be regarded as possible hedges against inflation (Wasserfallen, 1989). It would,

[5] The unexpected changes in the real interest is also a potential variable to be included in this study. However, as Chen and Jordan (1993) point out, because of the Fisher effect this variable is perfectly negatively correlated with the unexpected inflation rate, and was therefore not considered.

therefore, be of interest to potential investors in international industry portfolios, to find out whether global inflation can be hedged against.

Several studies include oil prices, as an important systematic factor, believed to influence stock returns. Chen et al (1986) study oil prices as a measure of economic risk in the U.S. market, whereas Hamao (1988) examines oil price risk in Japan. In this study, we use oil prices as a global potential source of risk, to which different international industries may have differing exposures.

There has been some empirical evidence on the significance of industrial production as discussed in chapters 6 and 7 in this book. Chen et al (1986) study the effect of US industrial production in the US market, while Hamao (1988), examines the same relationships using Japanese data. Poon and Taylor (1991) study the effects of unexpected changes in industrial production in the UK equity market. Only Ferson and Harvey (1993, 1994) examine the effects of global industrial output risks on various national equity markets. No study yet, however, has examined the effects of global industrial production in an international industry context.

The final macroeconomic factor included in the analysis, is a measure of global credit risk, UdTED. This variable captures the effects of the term structure of interest rates internationally and is included, because fluctuations in the spread may capture fluctuations in global industry returns. Ferson and Harvey (1994) consider the effect of the same variable on 18 national equity markets, but find no significant impact.

8.3 Data

Monthly price indices (with 1970:1 = 100) for 38 International Industries as calculated by Morgan Stanley Capital International (MSCI), and all the data series needed for the construction of the global macro variables are obtained from DataStream International Service for the period[6] 1986:3 - 1997:10.

[6] Data for the MSCI International Industry Indices are available from DataStream starting January 1982.

The MSCI price indices are value-weighted and aim for 60% coverage of the total market capitalisation for each market. Companies in the indices replicate the industry composition of each local market. The chosen list of stocks, formed from the share prices[7] of approximately 1600 securities in 22 countries, includes a representative sample of large, medium, and small capitalisation companies from each local market, taking into account the stocks' liquidity. Furthermore, stocks with restricted float or cross-ownership are avoided. Industry returns, $XR_{i,t}$, are calculated for each of the 38 global industry indices, as: $XR_{it} = \ln(I_{i,t}/I_{i,t-1})-R_f$, where I_{it}, I_{it-1} are the index values of industry i at time t and t-1 respectively, in $US, and R_f is the risk free rate of interest.

The explanatory variables entering equation (8.1) are defined as follows: WDRET is the U.S. dollar monthly logarithmic excess return on the MSCI World Index, where the 1-month U.S. Treasury Bill rate, USTB, is used as the risk-free rate. That is, $WDRET_t=\ln(PW_t/PW_{t-1})-USTB_t$, where PW_t is the world equity index value in $US. dG10FX is the monthly global exchange rate against the $US in 10 industrialised countries (G-10). It is derived by calculating the log first difference in the trade-weighted U.S. dollar price of the currencies of the 10 industrialised countries.[8,9] TLP is the real GDP weighted inflation rate in the G-7 countries. Country inflation rates are derived as logarithmic first differences of consumer price indices. dTED is the spread between the 3-month Eurodollar deposit rate and the 3-month U.S. Treasury Bill rate. This variable is a measure of the premium on Eurodollar deposit rates in London, relative to the U.S. Treasury. dOIL represents the percentage change in oil prices, the latter measured as the current month U.S. dollar price per barrel of Brent Oil (FOB). dG7IP is the weighted average of monthly industrial production growth rates in the G-7 countries, with real GDP as weights.

Table 8.1, shows the autocorrelations of the series (up to 12 lags) and the Box - Pierce Q-statistic (at lag 20) testing for 20th order autocorrelation in each series. It can be

[7] Share prices included in the indices are adjusted for any rights issues, stock dividends and/or splits.
[8] The 10 industrialised countries are the G-7 countries (excluding the United States), plus the Netherlands, Belgium, Sweden, and Switzerland. The G-7 countries are: Canada, France, Germany, Italy, Japan, the United Kingdom, and the United States.
[9] The trade weights are each country's U.S. dollar denominated FOB imports, expressed as a percentage of total imports in the G-10 countries.

seen that only WDRET is noisy enough to be treated as an innovation, whereas all the remaining five series are serially correlated.

Table 8.1: Autocorrelations of the Monthly Global Macroeconomic Series

SERIES	WDRET	TLP	DTED	DOIL	DG10FX	DG7IP	UTLP	UDTED	UDOIL	UDG10FX	UDG7IP
Lag 1	0.046	0.300*	0.836*	0.150*	-0.129*	-0.325*	0.0433	-0.0267	0.0738	-0.0703	0.0153
Lag 2	-0.141*	-0.118*	0.725*	-0.038	-0.278*	0.109	-0.088	-0.0246	-0.0987	-0.0936	0.0843
Lag 3	-0.127*	-0.149*	0.660*	-0.0367	0.0446	0.172*	-0.1	0.0328	-0.0418	-0.0182	0.0862
Lag 4	-0.121*	0.0053	0.623*	-0.197*	0.0252	0.0048	0.024	-0.0244	-0.0234	-0.121	0.105
Lag 5	0.0738	0.228*	0.628*	-0.293*	-0.0574	0.0605	0.041	-0.1	-0.0083	-0.0178	0.0957
Lag 6	-0.0472	0.260*	0.644*	-0.14	0.0433	0.0798	-0.144	0.0681	0.0264	0.0302	0.00735
Lag 7	-0.0005	0.227*	0.626*	-0.105	-0.145*	-0.132	0.066	0.117	-0.106	-0.123	-0.0813
Lag 8	0.0349	0.0565	0.557*	0.0733	0.150*	0.083	0.09	-0.0963	0.0161	0.106	0.0956
Lag 9	0.0756	-0.0507	0.527*	0.103	0.056	0.153	0.082	0.0506	-0.0527	-0.0568	0.152
Lag 10	0.162*	-0.0754	0.486	0.109	-0.294*	-0.144	-0.026	-0.0347	-0.0764	0.0137	-0.059
Lag 11	-0.0912	0.208	0.462	0.0966	-0.0244	0.105	0.025	-0.128	-0.024	0.0141	0.0987
Lag 12	-0.0777	0.5430*	0.484	0.0608	0.407*	0.107	0.028	0.0663	0.026	-0.0988	0.1100*
Q-statistic (lag 20)	29.2	128*	837*	51.6*	73.9*	50.3*	21.8	13.3	12.8	21.6	22.9

Notes: 1. Sample autocorrelations of up to order 12 and the Box - Pierce Q-statistic for 20 lags, testing for 20th order serial correlation in the series are shown. 2. WDRET is the return on the M.S.C.I. World Equity Index, TLP is the G-7 inflation rate, dTED is the Eurodollar - Treasury spread, dOIL represents changes in the U.S. dollar price per barrel of Brent Oil, dG10FX is the G-10 aggregate exchange rate against the U.S. dollar, and dG7IP is monthly industrial production in the G-7 countries. UTLP, UdTED, UdOIL, UdG10FX, and UdG7IP are the unexpected components of TLP, dTED, dOIL, dG10FX, and dG7IP, respectively. 3. * and ** indicate significance at the 5%, and 10% level respectively.

Based on the investigation of AIC and SBIC criteria the best ARMA model is chosen for each series TLP, dTED, dOIL, dG10FX, and dG7IP, and the residuals from the fitted processes are used to proxy the unanticipated components of these series. Parameters of the ARMA models employed are displayed in table 8.2. Autocorrelations and Q-statistics associated with these new variables confirm that the series are white noise. These new variables created, UTLP, UdTED, UdOIL, UdG10FX, and UdG7IP, are used as explanatory variables in estimating equation (8.1) for 38 international industries using Ordinary Least Squares (OLS), for the period 1987:3 1997:10.

Table 8.3, presents the contemporaneous correlation matrix of the global risk factors used in equation (8.1), in order to examine the possibility of collinearity between the explanatory variables of the model. The only significant correlation is that between WDRET and UdTED (-0.2926), indicating that multi-collinearity is not a potential problem in the estimated model.

Table 8.2: Estimated 'best' ARMA model for each variable

SERIES	TLP	DTED	DOIL	DG10FX	DG7IP
Constant	0.0005	0	0.0021	0.0003	0.0025*
Lag 1	0.2026*	0.7228*	-	-	-0.3552*
Lag 3	-	-	-	-	0.1773*
Lag 4	-	-	-0.1437**	-	-
Lag 5	-	0.1809*	-0.2422*	-	-
Lag 6	0.1452**	-	-0.1341**	-	-
Lag 10	-	-	-	-0.1899*	-
Lag 12	0.4203*	-	-	0.3986	-
AIC	-9.7276	-14.3305	-1.9477	-3.7465	-7.2754
SBIC	-12.4764	-17.1016	-4.6964	-6.5176	-10.0465

Notes: 1. TLP is the G-7 inflation rate, dTED is the Eurodollar - Treasury spread, dOIL represents changes in the U.S. dollar price per barrel of Brent Oil, dG10FX is the G-10 aggregate exchange rate against the U.S. dollar, and dG7IP is monthly industrial production in the G-7 countries. 2. * and ** indicate significance at the 1%, and 5% level respectively. 3. Non-significant lags are not reported. 4. AIC is the Akaike Information Criterion and the SBIC is the Schwarz Bayesian Information Criterion

Table 8.3: Correlation Matrix of the World Risk Factors

VARIABLE	WDRET	UDTED	UDOIL	UDG10FX	UDG7IP	UTLP
WDRET	1.000					
UdTED	-0.2926*	1.000				
UdOIL	-0.0356	0.1441	1.000			
UdG10FX	-0.0323	-0.0264	-0.0967	1.000		
UdG7IP	0.00916	0.0056	0.0661	-0.0528	1.000	
UTLP	0.0443	-0.0368	0.0605	-0.0396	-0.0005	1.000

Notes: 1. See Table 8.1 for definitions of WDRET, UdTED, UdOIL, UdG10FX, UdG7IP, and UTLP. * indicates significance at the 5% level.

8.4 Empirical Tests and Results

The effects of the innovations in macroeconomic factors on each international industry return, estimated through equation (8.1), are shown in table 8.4. In order to select the 'best' model for each of the 38 industries the general-to-specific modelling approach is adopted. It involves starting from the most general model with all the variables included and allowing the data to determine which variables are significant. The approach avoids the possible omitted variables bias problems that may arise otherwise.

Table 8.4: Coefficients of the global risk variables; period 1987:3-1997:10

M.S.C.I. INTERNATIONAL INDUSTRIES	CONST	WDRET	UDTED	UDOIL	UDG10FX	UDG7IP	UTLP	R^2-ADJ. MACRO FACT	R^2-ADJ. ONLY WDRET
AEROSPACE & MILITARY TECH.	0.027	0.8524✣		-0.0715✣				0.477	0.465
APPLIANCES & HOUSEHOLD DURABLES	-0.017	1.1491✣						0.532	
AUTOMOBILES	-0.011	1.0236✣				0.6168♦		0.659	0.656
BANKING	-0.014	1.1974✣						0.699	
BEVERAGES & TOBACCO	0.049♦	0.8141✣						0.568	
BROADCASTING & PUBLISHING	0.007	0.8589✣		-0.0549*				0.537	0.530
BUILDING MATERIALS & COMPONENTS	-0.04♦	1.1177✣						0.764	
BUSINESS & PUBLIC SERVICES	0.003	0.8992✣		-0.0445*			-1.4845♦	0.766	0.756
CHEMICALS	-0.001	1.0662✣						0.827	
CONS. & HOUSING	-0.01♦	1.2758✣						0.472	
DATA PROCESSING & REPRODUCTION	-0.004	0.9164✣						0.394	
ELECTRICAL & ELECTRONICS	0.002	0.9757✣						0.683	
ELECTRONIC COMPONENTS & INSTRUMENTS	0.006	1.0736✣					-3.6217*	0.440	0.435
ENERGY EQUIPMENT & SERVICES	0.002	0.9714✣		0.171✣				0.384	0.336
ENERGY SOURCES	0.002	0.7323✣	-27.432*	0.181✣				0.664	0.521
FOOD & HOUSEHOLD PRODUCTS	0.002	0.7958✣			0.0778♦			0.730	0.727
FOREST PRODUCTS & PAPER	-0.003	0.9399✣					2.7656♦	0.611	0.603
INDUSTRIAL COMPONENTS	-0.001	1.1133✣						0.807	
INSURANCE	0.000	0.8927✣		-0.0419*				0.764	0.758
FINANCIAL SERVICES	-0.005	1.6262✣						0.714	
GOLD MINES	-0.005	0.6704✣					10.471✣	0.122	0.086
HEALTH & PERSONAL CARE	0.006*	0.8189✣						0.603	
LEISURE & TOURISM	0.002	0.9792✣		-0.0575*				0.657	0.649
MACHINERY & ENGINEERING	-0.001	1.2176✣				0.6867♦		0.780	0.776
MERCHANDISING	0.002	0.9169✣		-0.0572*				0.723	0.712
METALS-NON FERROUS	-0.001	1.0756✣					6.5857✣	0.472	0.443
METALS- STEEL	-0.004	1.2889✣				1.5898*		0.425	0.415
MISC. MATERIALS & COMMODITIES	-0.004♦	1.2549✣	27.21*		-0.085♦		1.7696♦	0.792	0.782
MULTI INDUSTRY	0.001	0.9891✣					2.8297*	0.657	0.652
REAL ESTATE	-0.002	1.3400✣						0.688	
RECREATION & OTHER GOODS	-0.001	0.8892✣		0.0533*				0.600	0.593
TELECOMMUNICATIONS	0.001	0.6789✣						0.531	0.526
TEXTILES & APPAREL	-0.006*	1.2211✣			-0.2538✣			0.735	0.712
TRANSPORTATION- AIRLINES	-0.003	1.0983✣		-0.0796✣				0.641	0.628
TRANSPORTATION- ROAD & RAIL	-0.005	1.1765✣						0.584	
TRANSPORTATION- SHIPPING	-0.001	1.2067✣						0.607	
UTILITIES- ELECTRICAL & GAS	-0.001	0.7065✣	-33.67✣		0.1062♦		-3.8665✣	0.599	0.546
WHOLESALE & INTERNATIONAL TRADE	-0.007	1.5454✣						0.560	

Notes: 1. ✣, * and ♦ indicate significance at the 1%, 5%, and 10% level respectively. 2. See Table 8.1 for definitions of WDRET, UdTED, UdOIL, UdG10FX, UdG7IP, and UTLP. 3. N=128 is the number of observations for each M.S.C.I. international industry.

A significantly positive constant for an industry indicates that excess returns in this industry have, on average, been positive during the sample period indicating under-pricing, and vice-versa for significantly negative constants. This is the case for only 6 out of 38 industries, and 4 out of these 6 industries have significant negative coefficients, indicating overpricing of stocks.

The global market risk factor, WDRET, is significant and positive in every industry. The same, however, cannot be said about the effect of other macroeconomic risk factors. Several significant relationships are established, however, the impact of each macroeconomic factor differs across industries. This can be attributed to the fact that effects of macroeconomic events are subject to characteristics specific to an industry, as noted above. This important finding is in line with other evidence presented in earlier chapters of this book. Therefore, there is no systematic way in which the macroeconomy affects returns across industries either at the national or global levels.

UdTED is a measure of global credit risk. Empirical evidence on the effects of this factor on stock returns is rather limited. Ferson and Harvey (1994) include the same variable in their study, but find that it has no significant effect on the returns of 18 national equity indices. In this paper, though, UdTED is found to have a significant long run effect on the returns of only 3 industries at the international level. Sectors where the variable has a negative effect, are the Energy Sources and the Utilities industries. The factor positively affects stock returns in the Miscellaneous Materials & Commodities industry.

Many studies in the past have examined the effects of oil prices, UdOIL, on stock returns. Findings have, however, been contradicting. Chen and Jordan (1993) for example find that oil prices are negatively related to stock returns in the US, while Chen et al (1986), find no significant relationship. Our results are more in line with findings in chapters 6 and 7 of this book, where it is oil prices appear significant and have varying effects on different industry sectors. The Energy Sources international industry index, for instance, is positively related to changes in the price of Brent Oil. In this case, the positive relationship is justified, because rising oil prices imply a higher return for energy companies. In contrast, oil prices are negatively related to stock returns in the Airline Transportation industry. This negative relationship is again justified on the grounds that higher oil prices imply higher costs and therefore lower returns in this industry.

UdG10FX, the foreign exchange risk factor, has also been found to have varying effects across stocks of the four international industries for which it appears to be significant. Empirical evidence regarding this factor is not conclusive either. Dumas and Solnik (1995), using a sample of securities that includes equities and currencies, present results that support the existence of time-varying foreign exchange risk premia in the international financial markets. Ziobrowski and Ziobrowski (1995) reach similar conclusions in an international context. Hamao (1988) finds that unanticipated changes in foreign exchange do not explain the cross-section of stocks listed in the Tokyo Stock Exchange. In contrast, Ferson and Harvey (1994), using a similar aggregate measure of exchange risk as in this paper, found a significant average risk premium.

When the coefficients of this variable are positive, a dollar depreciation implies higher returns, since exchange rates are measured in U.S. dollars per national currency units. The opposite holds when the coefficients of the variable are found to negatively affect returns. Examples of sectors that benefit from a dollar depreciation - a positive coefficient - are those of Food & Household Products and the Utilities industries, whereas sectors such as the Miscellaneous Materials & Commodities and the Textiles & Apparel industries exhibit a negative relationship to this measure of foreign exchange risk, i.e. when the dollar depreciates, equity returns in these sectors are lower.

Monthly global industrial production is found to positively affect the stock returns of 3 industries. Financial theory regarding this variable suggests a positive association with stock returns, on the grounds that higher industrial production implies improving economic conditions and therefore higher stock returns. Empirical evidence is, however, inconclusive. Poon and Taylor (1991) find a negative effect of industrial production in the UK, in line with chapters 6 and 7 of this book, while Chen and Jordan (1993) find no association between the variable and stock returns. The sectors which are positively related to unexpected changes in industrial production are the Automobiles, the Machinery & Engineering Sectors and the Steel industries.

In the case of unexpected inflation, UTLP, the pattern that emerges is not uniform. The factor has a significant impact on the stock returns of 8 industries. In 3 of them the effect is negative, namely the Business & Public Services, the Electronics Components & Instrument and the Utilities industry sectors. The bulk of empirical evidence suggests that inflation is negatively related to stock returns in many countries (e.g. Gultekin (1983) and Chen et al (1986)). This is rather surprising, because asset returns should provide a protection against inflation. Following this intuition, industries whose stocks exhibit a positive relationship with UTLP - e.g. Gold Mines, Non-Ferrous Metals - can be regarded as hedges against inflation (Wasserfallen (1989)).

Comparison of the adjusted-R^2 in table 8.4, from the single factor model - where the market index, WDRET, is the only explanatory factor - with the corresponding statistic from the multifactor model seems to indicate that the excess return on the market portfolio is the most important factor in explaining returns. However, the inclusion of other macrovariables increases the explanatory power of the model only marginally. These findings are in line with past empirical evidence (e.g. Ferson and Harvey (1994)).

According to the results based on the multifactor model, the riskiest industries, with respect to WDRET, appear to be the Financial Services, Wholesale & International Trade and the Real Estate industry sectors. On the other hand, the least risky industries are the Gold Mines, Telecommunications and the Energy Sources industries.

8.5 Summary and Conclusion

This is the first study to examine the long run impacts of several sources of global risk on the excess returns of 38 international industries, as defined by Morgan Stanley Capital International (MSCI). A multi factor time series model is employed, including innovations in the following pre-specified set of global macroeconomic factors: 1) the return on the MSCI World Equity Index, 2) the Eurodollar-Treasury yield spread, 3) oil prices, 4) an aggregate measure of exchange rate risk, 5) industrial production, and 6) inflation.

Among the factors considered, the return of the world market portfolio affects significantly all the 38 international industries under analysis. It is by far the most important factor in explaining the variation in international industry returns. Inclusion of macroeconomic factors marginally increases the explanatory power of the model. Several significant relationships are detected with respect to the remaining factors that do not, generally, exhibit a consistent pattern in the way in which they affect returns of global industries. The long run impact a factor may have, can be positive on the returns of a particular industry, and negative or insignificant on the returns of another, depending on industry specific characteristics.

The fact that world capital markets are becoming increasingly more integrated with companies operating across borders, forming alliances/mergers in several industrial sectors, suggests that the degree of integration in industries is such that global asset management firms increasingly place an industry focus in their research. Moreover, given this industry integration or segmentation in the world economy, evidence on the sources of risk that may affect stock returns across industries at the international level is of primary importance in adopting an optimal strategy for global investing.

The practical implications of this study, therefore, for portfolio managers are important. The industrial classification of a given asset becomes crucial, as certain global industries develop to be homogeneous, and capital markets are becoming increasingly integrated. The significant relationships between global macroeconomic factors and international industry stock returns detected in this paper, are useful to the investor who can exploit these relationships in order to increase his diversification capacity or speculate by timing his investment. Whether or not, however, these global sources of risk are actually priced (in a cross-section study) in the international financial market is a question of future research.

CHAPTER 9: CONCLUSION

9.1. Major Findings of the Book

The aim of this section is to discuss the major findings of the book. Before embarking on the actual discussion of the findings, we feel it would be helpful to present them, in tabular form, so that the reader can obtain a full picture of the major findings of the research. This is done in table 9.1.

Table 9.1: The Major Findings of this Book

Chapter 4: Risk and return of U.S. water transportation stocks over time and over bull and bear market conditions

Period Covered: January 1985 - December 1994
Methodology: CAPM
Major Findings:

- Industry Average Beta: 0.9199 (= 1)
- Industry Average Alpha: 0.00218 (> 0)
- Parameters exhibit stability over time
- No constant "size effect" over time
- Shift of alpha, but not beta, over bull and bear market conditions

Note: Figures in parenthesis indicate statistical equality or non-equality to the number in parenthesis

Beta comparisons across industries - A water transportation industry perspective

Period Covered: July 1984 - June 1995
Methodology: CAPM
Major Findings:

- **Industry CAPM Parameters**

Industry	Alpha	Beta
Water Transportation	0.0352 (> 0)	0.9411 (< 1)
Air Transportation	0.0124 (> 0)	0.9748 (= 1)
Rail Transportation	0.0150 (> 0)	1.0155 (= 1)
Trucks	0.0206 (> 0)	0.9676 (= 1)
Electricity	0.0668 (> 0)	0.9465 (< 1)
Gas	0.0447 (> 0)	0.9581 (< 1)
Petroleum Refining	0.0039 (> 0)	0.9838 (= 1)
Real Estate	0.0260 (> 0)	0.6933 (< 1)

- The beta of the water transportation industry is significantly lower than the beta of the rail transportation industry and significantly higher than the beta of the real estate industry.

Note: Figures in parenthesis indicate statistical equality or non-equality to the number in parenthesis

Chapter 5: Microeconomic Factors as Determinants of Equity Returns

Period Covered: July 1984 - June 1995
Methodology: Multifactor Model employing fundamental microeconomic factors
Major Findings:

- Industry Multifactor Model Parameters

Industry	Alpha	Beta	ME	B/M	A/ME	A/BE	E/P[1]
Water Transportation	0.0420 (> 0)	0.9410 (< 1)				-	
Air Transportation	0.0030 (> 0)	0.9760 (= 1)				-	
Rail Transportation	0.0080 (> 0)	1.0110 (= 1)			+		
Trucks	0.0210 (> 0)	0.9680 (= 1)					
Electricity	0.0770 (> 0)	0.9420 (< 1)		+			
Gas	0.0650 (> 0)	0.9520 (< 1)	-				
Petroleum Refining	0.0230 (> 0)	0.9760 (= 1)	+		+	-	
Real Estate	0.0280 (> 0)	0.6890 (< 1)		+			

- The beta of the water transportation industry is significantly lower than the beta of the rail transportation industry and significantly higher than the beta of the real estate industry.
- The only industry beta which exhibits significant temporal variability is that of the petroleum refining industry. In the water transportation and the other six industries no significant temporal change has occurred.

Notes: 1. Figures in parenthesis indicate statistical equality or non-equality to the number in the parenthesis. 2. Where the sign is positive, this means that there is a positive relationship between that factor and returns. Where the sign is negative, the opposite holds. The magnitude of each factor is discussed in detail in the relevant chapter. Where no sign appears, the coefficient is statistically insignificant.

Chapter 6: Macroeconomic Factors as Determinants of Equity Returns

Period Covered: July 1985 - June 1995
Methodology: Multifactor Model employing macroeconomic factors
Major Findings:

- Industry Multifactor Model Parameters

Industry	Alpha	Beta	UMIP	UTS	UOG	UCG	UI[2]
Water Transportation	0.0346 (> 0)	0.9449 (< 1)	-		+		
Air Transportation	0.0103 (> 0)	0.9538 (= 1)		+			
Rail Transportation	0.0289 (> 0)	0.9875 (= 1)				-	
Trucks	0.0176 (> 0)	0.9698 (= 1)		+	-		
Electricity	0.0642 (> 0)	0.9248 (< 1)	-	-			
Gas	0.0426 (> 0)	0.9579 (< 1)			+	-	
Petroleum Refining	0.0320 (> 0)	0.9741 (= 1)		+	+		
Real Estate	0.0348 (> 0)	0.7543 (< 1)			-		

- The beta of the water transportation industry is not significantly different to the beta of any other transportation or non- - transportation industry.

Notes: 1. Figures in parenthesis indicate statistical equality or non-equality to the number in the parenthesis. 2. Where the sign is positive, this means that there is a positive relationship between that factor and returns. Where the sign is negative, the opposite holds. The magnitude of each factor is discussed in detail in the relevant chapter. Where no sign appears, the coefficient is statistically insignificant.

[1] ME, B/M, A/ME, A/BE and E/P correspond to market value of equity, book to market, total assets to market equity, total assets to book equity and earnings to price ratios respectively.
[2] UMIP, UTS, UOG, UCG, UI correspond to unanticipated changes in monthly industrial production, the term structure, oil prices, consumption and inflation respectively.

Chapter 7: Microeconomic and Macroeconomic Factors - A Unified Approach

Period Covered: July 1985 - June 1995
Methodology: Multifactor Model employing both micro and macroeconomic factors
Major Findings:

- Industry Multifactor Model Parameters:

Industry	Alpha	Beta	UMIP	UTS	UOG	UCG	UI
Water Transportation	0.0334 (> 0)	0.9438 (< 1)	-		+		
Air Transportation	0.0206 (> 0)	0.9471 (= 1)		+	-		
Rail Transportation	0.0289 (> 0)	0.9878 (= 1)				-	
Trucks	0.0228 (> 0)	0.9593 (= 1)		+	-		
Electricity	0.0710 (> 0)	0.9264 (< 1)	-	-			
Gas	0.0603 (> 0)	0.9580 (< 1)			+	-	
Petroleum Refining	0.0197 (> 0)	0.9676 (= 1)		+	+		
Real Estate	0.0348 (> 0)	0.7543 (< 1)			-		

Industry	ME	B/M	A/ME	A/BE	E/P
Water Transportation	+			-	
Air Transportation				-	
Rail Transportation					
Trucks					
Electricity		+			
Gas	-				
Petroleum Refining	+		+	-	
Real Estate					

- The beta of the water transportation industry is not significantly different to the beta of any other transportation or non- - transportation industry.

Notes: 1. Figures in parenthesis indicate statistical equality or non-equality to the number in the parenthesis. 2. Where the sign is positive, this means that there is a positive relationship between that factor and returns. Where the sign is negative, the opposite holds. The magnitude of each factor is discussed in detail in the relevant chapter. Where no sign appears, the coefficient is statistically insignificant.

Chapter 8: Macroeconomic Factors and International Industry Returns

Period Covered: March 1987 – October 1997
Methodology: Multifactor Model employing global macroeconomic factors
Major Findings: See Table 8.4 in chapter 8.

Having presented a summary of the results of chapters 4 – 8 in table 9.1, we now proceed with the presentation, again in tabular form, of empirical evidence regarding the micro (table 9.2.A) and macroeconomic (table 9.2.B) factors employed in this book for the US industries. We list other studies similar to ours, which have also attempted to identify the determinants of stock returns by using sets of either microeconomic or macroeconomic factors. This is done in order to compare the findings of this book with other relevant literature we have seen in the past. However, when comparing the results, it should be kept in mind that the majority of published work utilises a wide sample of companies, which have used portfolios as a basis for asset pricing rather than industry classification, as in our study.

Table 9.2.A: Empirical Evidence regarding the Macroeconomic Factors employed in this Book for the US

Factor Employed	Study	Findings of Study	Findings of this Book	Applicable Industry
Unanticipated Monthly growth of Industrial Production	Poon and Taylor (1991)	- ve effect	-ve effect	Water Transportation
	Bong - Soo Lee (1992)	+ ve effect	-ve effect	Electricity
	Chen, Roll and Ross (1986)	+ ve effect		
	Pearce and Roley (1985)	n.s.		
	Chen and Jordan (1993)	n.s.		
Unanticipated changes in term structure	Chen, Roll and Ross (1986)	+ ve effect	+ve effect	Air Transportation
	Poon and Taylor (1991)	n.s.	+ve effect	Trucks
	Chen and Jordan (1993)	n.s.	+ve effect	Petroleum Refining
			- ve effect	Electricity
Unanticipated changes in oil prices	Chen, Roll and Ross (1986)	+ ve effect	+ve effect	Water Transportation
	Chen and Jordan (1993)	- ve effect	+ve effect	Gas
			+ve effect	Petroleum Refining
			- ve effect	Trucks
			- ve effect	Real Estate
Unanticipated changes in consumption	Rubinstein (1976)	+ ve effect	- ve effect	Rail Transportation
	Lucas (1978)	+ ve effect	- ve effect	Gas
	Breeden (1979)	+ ve effect		
	Wasserfallen (1989)	- ve effect		
Unanticipated Inflation	Chen, Roll and Ross (1986)	- ve effect	n.s.	All industries
	Hamao (1988)	- ve effect		
	Wasserfallen (1989)	- ve effect		
	Poon and Taylor (1991)	n.s.		
	Martinez and Rubio (1989)	n.s.		

Table 9.2.B: Empirical Evidence regarding the Microeconomic Factors employed in this Book for the US

Factor Employed	Study	Findings of Study	Findings of this Book	Applicable Industry
Market value of Equity	Banz (1981)	- ve effect	+ ve effect	Water Transportation
	Basu (1977, 1983)	- ve effect	+ ve effect	Petroleum Refining
	Reinganum (1981)	- ve effect	- ve effect	Gas
	Lakonishok and Shapiro (1986)	- ve effect		
	Fama and French (1992)	- ve effect		
Book to Market value of Equity	Stattman (1980)	+ ve effect	+ve effect	Electricity
	Rosenberg et al. (1985)	+ ve effect	+ve effect	Real Estate
	Fama and French (1992)	+ ve effect		
	Chen et al. (1991)	+ ve effect		
Asset to market value of Equity	Fama and French (1992)	+ ve effect	+ve effect	Rail Transportation
	Bhandari (1988)	+ ve effect	+ve effect	Petroleum Refining
Asset to book value of Equity	Fama and French (1992)	- ve effect	- ve effect	WaterTransportation
			- ve effect	Air Transportation
			- ve effect	Petroleum Refining
Earnings to Price	Ball (1978)	+ ve effect	n.s.	All industries
	Reinganum (1981)	+ ve effect		
	Basu (1983)	+ ve effect		
	Fama and French (1992)	n.s.		

As can be seen from the two tables, there are similarities as well as differences among the results of this book and the general literature. Most differences show up with respect to the macroeconomic factors which, incidentally, tend to also exhibit differences across other empirical studies.

The major difference obtained regarding microeconomic factors is that of size, where the evidence in the financial literature suggests a negative effect. In the case of this book, it appears that in the majority of the industries where a "size effect" is documented it is of a positive sign. This might be due to the fact that the analysis undertaken in this study is carried out at industry level and not utilising the full universe of stocks. It appears that in a number of the industries analysed, larger companies tend to outperform smaller ones.

9.1.1. Summary of Results from the CAPM: Intertemporal Analysis, Different market conditions and Cross Industry Comparison

The results of chapter 4 indicate a number of interesting aspects regarding the behaviour of water transportation company stocks during the period 1985 to 1994. Firstly, the average beta of shipping companies was estimated to be numerically lower but not statistically different from the beta of the "average" company (unity). This result of the systematic, non- - diversifiable, risk of the water transportation industry not being different from the average market risk could make the shipping industry an attractive candidate for potential investors. Furthermore, another attractive characteristic of the beta coefficient of the water transportation industry, from the investor's point of view, is the fact that it appears to be stable over time.

Secondly, water transportation companies appear, with some notable exceptions, not to be underpriced over the full ten-year period examined. Sub-period estimations of the CAPM coefficients suggest that underpricing did not occur during the first five-year period as well as during the second five-year period.

Thirdly, there appears to be a "size" effect in the shipping industry for the period 1984-1989 in the sense that smaller shipping companies tend to exhibit higher returns. These higher returns, as might be expected, were found to be accompanied both by higher total and systematic risk. However, this "size" effect disappears in the period 1990 - 1994 possibly due to the shifting of several "small" caps to the medium and large groupings.

This chapter also examines whether underpricing, as measured by alpha, or the systematic risk, as measured by beta, of the water transportation companies included in the sample examined changed over bull and bear market conditions during the ten year period examined. It is found that alpha, not beta, tends to be mostly affected by upward or downward market movements. Therefore, investors considering including shipping stocks in their portfolios need not worry about possible changes in the systematic risk of these stocks during changing market conditions.

Another aim of this chapter is to examine the risk-return relationship of the water transportation industry along another dimension, that of comparing the systematic risk of companies belonging to this industry to the systematic risk of companies belonging to other related and non - related industries. In this context, the beta of the water transportation industry is compared to the beta of the following seven industries: rail transportation; air transportation; trucks; electricity; petroleum refining; gas and; real estate. To achieve that, the Capital Asset Pricing Model is employed.

Results reveal some further interesting characteristics of the stock returns of the water transportation industry in the U.S. during the period 1984 - 1995. The beta of the water transportation industry is significantly lower than the beta of the rail transportation industry and the beta of the real estate industry. It is statistically similar to the betas of the five other industries employed in the chapter.

Looking at the findings of this chapter, one might conclude that stocks belonging to the water transportation industry do not appear to possess any risk characteristic the investment community is not aware of. The industry average beta of 0.92 seems to be in line with the average company's beta, unity, and the average explanatory power of the regressions of around 23% is also typical in these kind of estimations. Furthermore, tests suggesting that the industry beta does not appear to change over time, despite the cyclical nature of the underlying industry, can only be "good" news for the industry's stock market perception. Moreover, numerically speaking, the beta of the water transportation industry is the lowest of all transportation industries' betas.

9.1.2. Microeconomic Factors as Determinants of Equity Returns

Chapter 5 undertakes a comparative analysis of the stock market perception of the risk-return relationship of US listed water transportation stocks in relation to stocks belonging to the other transportation and non-transportation sectors mentioned above over the same time period. The significant difference between this analysis and the one in chapter 4 is that this one is carried out in a multidimensional risk environment. More specifically, apart from relating cross-sectional differences in the returns of companies belonging to different sectors to the market, the model used in this chapter relates those differences to a number of fundamental, company specific, factors, which according to intuition and academic research are believed to influence stock returns. These factors are: the market value of equity (size), the book - to - market value of equity ratio; the earnings - to - price ratio; the asset - to - market value of equity ratio; and the asset - to - book value of equity.

SURE methods are used to estimate the relationship for each industry due to it possessing two significant advantages over the classic OLS. The first is that the sensitivities of each company's returns to the market (betas) are estimated simultaneously across companies together with the impact of the fundamental variables and the alphas also allowing the imposition of cross-equation restrictions on the parameters. The second is that the SURE, in contrast to more classic methodologies utilised in the past in similar studies, adjusts for the cross-sectional correlation in the residual returns across companies. This leads to parameter estimates which are more efficient than those given by OLS models, the gain being proportional to the correlation between disturbances from the different equations. This advantage is particularly important in studies of this nature since companies grouped according to their industry classification are likely to exhibit residual returns' correlation.

The results of the study indicate that there appear to be factors, from the microeconomic, company specific environment, which, in addition to the market (which remains the driving force behind returns), tend to influence the returns of the water transportation industry and the other industries. As might be observed from the table at the beginning of this section, the significance of the fundamental variables appears to vary across sectors and over time. The book-to-market value, the asset-to-market and the asset-to-book value of equity ratios, and the market value of equity are significant in some industries but not in others while the earnings-to-price ratio has no role to play in any industry's returns. Generally speaking, the coefficients of the fundamental variables come out with the expected sign, save the positive "size effect" in the petroleum industry.

The returns of the water transportation industry appear to be influenced by only one factor, the asset-to-book value of equity ratio. The relationship is a negative one and suggests that as shipping companies become more highly geared, in terms of book leverage, their stock market performance deteriorates.

As far as systematic risk (beta) is concerned and in line with the findings of chapter 4, the water transportation industry, along with three other non-transportation industries, exhibits lower than average systematic risk for the whole period studied as well as for the two subperiods. Furthermore, the beta of the water transportation industry, along with that of six other industries, does not vary from subperiod one to subperiod two while only the real estate industry exhibits a lower beta than the water transportation industry.

Finally, as in chapter 4, the alpha of the water transportation industry along with the alphas of all other industries analysed are positive thus suggesting that these industries have been underpriced over the time horizon studied.

9.1.3. Macroeconomic Factors as Determinants of Equity Returns

This, the sixth chapter of the book, is in the spirit of the fifth chapter in the sense that the traditional one - factor market model is augmented to include a number of other economic factors believed to influence security returns. However, in this chapter, the factors used are macroeconomic, as opposed to microeconomic used in the previous one. Hence, returns of companies in each industry are related to the stock market and the unexpected part of the following set of macroeconomic factors: industrial production, the term structure of interest rates, oil prices, consumption, and inflation. The selection of this set of macroeconomic factors was driven both by intuition, since the aforementioned factors affect both the future cash flows and riskiness of a company, as well as due to their popularity among academics (they have been widely used in previous studies).

MLSQ regression methods were used to estimate the relationship of the unanticipated changes in the above factors to the stock returns of each industry over the period 1985-1995. The results of this chapter, like the one preceding it, show that there are factors other than the market which influence the returns of the water transportation industry and other industries, thus justifying the use of multifactor models instead of the traditional one - factor, market model. More specifically, in line with the findings of chapters 4 and 5, the beta of the water transportation industry is found to be lower than the "average" beta of unity and it is also found to be among the lowest in the industries analysed. Moreover, the alpha of the water transportation industry, along with the alphas of the other industries analysed are significantly higher than zero thus implying that these industries have, on average, been underpriced over the period 1985 - 1995.

Regarding the macroeconomic factors, the authors find that their effect varies across industries. This is probably the most interesting and important finding of the study, that different industries tend to react differently to different economic shocks. The investment manager could utilise this finding, and by examining the sensitivities of industry stock returns to the macroeconomy, make better investment decisions.

As far as the returns of the water transportation industry are concerned, they appear to be influenced by two macroeconomic factors, monthly industrial production and oil prices. The former exerts a negative effect which suggests that increases in monthly industrial production are accompanied by dropping returns in the industry while the latter indicates a positive relationship which suggests that the returns of the water transportation industry are an increasing function of increases in oil prices.

Both of these findings appear to be against "conventional wisdom" and may be considered in the context of equation (1.2) in section 1.3 of chapter 1. As might be recalled, that equation expressed the value of a stock in terms of its future cash inflows discounted at an appropriate discount rate.

Irrespective of whether oil prices are an input or an output in an industry, oil prices affect the numerator of the aforementioned equation. If it is an input and the relevant industrial sector's capability to pass the full oil price increase to the consumer is limited, then the numerator of the equation and consequently the sector's valuation is affected negatively. If it is an output then it is likely that the numerator of the equation and the related sector's stock returns will increase. Hence, regarding the water transportation industry, rising oil prices might imply stockbuilding by several governments or large companies, a fact that might in turn imply increased demand for water transportation hence higher freight rates thus higher profits and subsequently better stock price performance.

9.1.4. Microeconomic and Macroeconomic Factors - A Unified Approach

The seventh chapter of the book combines the ideas discussed in chapters 5 and 6. The analysis in this chapter is done by relating cross-sectional differences in the returns of the companies in each of the industries mentioned in the previous chapters to the set of the microeconomic factors utilised in chapter 5 and the set of the macroeconomic factors utilised in chapter 6 simultaneously over the period 1985 - 1995.

This chapter recognises that both micro and macro economic factors may be determinants of stock returns across industries and attempts to uncover the determinants of each industry's stock returns in a more general setting where both sets of factors are included. As we have seen in section 1.3 of chapter 1, this practice is supported not only by academics (Fama and French (1992), Chen, Roll and Ross (1986) among others) but also by practitioners (BARRA).

Methodologically, given its advantages over OLS, SURE is used, as in chapter 5, since it provides more efficient estimates of the parameters of interest.

Results regarding market betas indicate that the market, as expected, has a significant role to play in explaining the returns of all industries. The beta of the water transportation industry is, as in the previous chapters, the lowest among the transportation industries and the third lowest, ranking behind electricity and gas, of all the industries analysed. Further inferences regarding market betas suggest that the market beta of the water transportation industry, along with the market betas of the electricity, gas and real estate industries, are significantly lower than the "average" market beta which is of course one.

Moreover, the alpha of the water transportation industry, along with the alphas of the other industries analysed are significantly higher than zero thus implying that these industries have, on average, been underpriced over the period 1985 - 1995.

As far as the economic factors are concerned, the returns of the water transportation industry were found to be positively related to oil prices and market value of equity and negatively related to monthly industrial production and the total assets-to-book value of equity ratio.

The sensitivities of each industry's returns to the set of microeconomic and macroeconomic factors, as expected, vary across industries. All factors, except the price to earnings ratio, appear to be priced in one industry or another. The estimation of this general model incorporating both microeconomic and macroeconomic factors for each industry sheds some light regarding differences both in the structure and sensitivities of each industry's stock returns to the set of factors employed.

At this point lies the first major usefulness of this analysis. The stock returns of the water transportation industry, for example, are positively affected by oil prices and the market value of equity and negatively affected by monthly industrial production and the asset-to-book value of equity. The aforementioned factors comprise a different set when compared to any other industry under analysis and hence the investment manager, by picking, or not picking, this industry, may expose, or not expose, his portfolio to the specific set of economic factors. The same holds of course for any other industry.

Furthermore, the industry analyst can also compare the direction and magnitude of the sensitivities of the different factors employed in the analysis to the returns of each industry. For example, an unanticipated change in oil prices affects the gas industry much more than the water transportation industry or the negative effect of market leverage is more profound in the electricity industry than in the water transportation industry.

Finally, it should be noted that the sign of the microeconomic and macroeconomic factors utilised is not always in line with the majority of the existing literature, thus pointing out that empirical results regarding the direction of the determinants of industry stock returns may differ, in some cases, to the direction of the determinants of the full universe of stocks. This is another important finding of this chapter and certainly an area, which could provide interesting research possibilities for the industry analyst.

9.1.5. Macroeconomic Factors and International Industry Returns - A Global Approach

Given that there is an increasing degree of integration in the capital markets internationally, an interesting question is the identification of factors affecting the risk / return profile across industries at the global level. This was done in chapter 8. Moreover, the industry focus that global asset management firms place in their research is of growing importance. In addition, the world economy is becoming increasingly more globalised with companies operating across borders, forming alliances/mergers in several industrial sectors, in some of them more than others. This industry internationalisation in the world economy requires investors to understand the factors affecting risk levels across companies at the international level. Any possible relationship between a set of prespecified global risk factors and fluctuations in international industry stock returns can be beneficial to the investor in the sense that he can increase his diversification capacity or even speculate by timing his investment.

The objective of this chapter was to present evidence for the first time, about the ability and the usefulness of world macroeconomic news in explaining the variability of global industry returns. The monthly risk variables employed in the study are: the excess return on a world equity market portfolio, fluctuations in global exchange rates, oil prices, global measures of inflation, industrial production growth and credit risk.

OLS regressions were used to estimate the relationship between unanticipated changes in the above factors and the excess returns of a set of 38 international industries, as compiled by Morgan Stanley Capital International (MSCI).

Among the factors considered, the return of the world market portfolio affects significantly all the 38 international industries under analysis. It is by far the most important factor in explaining the variation in international industry returns. Inclusion of macroeconomic factors marginally increases the explanatory power of the model. Several significant relationships are detected with respect to the remaining factors that do not, generally, exhibit a consistent pattern in the way in which they affect returns of global industries. The long run impact a factor may have, can be positive on the returns of a particular industry, and negative or insignificant on the returns of another, depending on industry specific characteristics. This finding is also consistent with evidence presented in chapters 6 and 7.

The practical implications of this study are important for portfolio managers. The industry integration or segmentation in the world economy, makes any evidence on the sources of risk that may affect stock returns across industries at the international level essential in adopting an optimal strategy for global investing.

The industrial classification of a given asset becomes crucial, as certain global industries develop to be homogeneous, and capital markets are becoming increasingly integrated. The significant relationships between global macroeconomic factors and international industry stock returns detected in this chapter, are useful to the investor who can exploit these relationships in order to increase his diversification capacity or speculate by timing his investment.

9.2. Usefulness of the Findings of this Book

Having reviewed and presented the most important findings of this book we discuss their usefulness which, up to a point at least, must be apparent by now. The findings of this book, might be useful for several groups of the investment community such as investors and portfolio managers as well as corporate financiers. This discussion is divided into two sections. Section 9.2.1 deals with the usefulness of the findings of the study for investors and portfolio managers while section 9.2.2 deals with its usefulness for the corporate financier.

9.2.1. Usefulness of the Findings for Investors and Portfolio Managers

Traditionally, investors and portfolio managers' strategies, regarding stock selection, are perceived as the choice of the proper mix of stocks in order to maximise returns subject to their risk profile. In order to achieve that however, they would need to identify what `features' really matter in a stock's or an industrial sector's performance. This book answers this question by expressing the returns of the eight industries analysed as a linear combination of each industry's returns' sensitivity to a number of microeconomic and macroeconomic factors times the risk premium on this factor.

As presented in section 9.1, every industrial sector analysed has its own pattern of sensitivities to the different microeconomic and macroeconomic factors employed. This might be used by the architect of the portfolio's investment strategy to determine the most desirable exposure to each risk factor. Altering the mix of industries included in the portfolio will certainly affect the amount, and type, of risk exposure to each factor studied. For example, suppose the portfolio manager wishes to move away from any unanticipated change in the term structure risk (an unanticipated widening or narrowing of the long vs short -term interest rates) since he believes that there will be some turbulence in the future regarding this factor. Utilising the multifactor model of chapter 7, he could exclude the air transportation, trucks, electricity and petroleum refining industries from his portfolio.

Alternatively, the portfolio manager could employ the above model to analyse the sensitivities of the factors employed to the returns of each industry. For example, for the water transportation industry the model would look as follows:

$$\textit{Excess Returns} = 0.0334 + 0.9438\, xXR_M + 0.0037\, xME - 0.0064\, xA/BE - 0.5846\, xUMIP + 0.0406xUOG$$

Using the above equation, the investment manager can substitute his expectations of each microeconomic and macroeconomic factor employed in order to arrive at the expected returns of the water transportation industry. Then, according to the confidence that he may be able to place in his expectations, he can decide upon the proportion of stocks that belong to this industry that he will include in his portfolio.

Furthermore, by comparing the above model to the corresponding models of the other industries analysed, the portfolio manager can diversify, more effectively, his risk with respect to the factors employed. Consider for example, the model for the air transportation industry:

$$\textit{Excess Returns} = 0.0206 + 0.9471\, x\, XR_M - 0.0153\, x\, A/BE + 0.1801\, x\, UTS - 0.0931\, x\, UOG$$

If the investment manager includes the air transportation industry in his portfolio, assuming that he has already included the water transportation industry in it, then he hedges for negative movements in oil prices. However, one could note that the negative exposure to oil prices is now larger than the positive one due to the fact that the negative coefficient of the air transportation industry is bigger than the positive coefficient of the water transportation industry. Here of course lies the art of portfolio architecture since it is up to the portfolio manager to decide what level of risk, for each factor, he is willing to take.

A closer look at table 7.1 reveals that the hedging process described above is more applicable with regards the macroeconomic factors since the microeconomic factors tend to behave similarly across industries. The issue regarding those then is to combine industries in such a way so as to obtain the required exposure to the given microeconomic factors employed. For example, consider now the model for the water transportation industry, the model for the air transportation industry and the model for the petroleum refining industry presented below:

$$\text{Excess Returns} = 0.0197 + 0.9676 \times XR_M + 0.0023 \times ME + 0.0327 \times A/ME - 0.0140 \times A/BE + 0.1025 \times UTS + 0.1662 \times UOG$$

Assume now that the investment manager believes that asset-to-book ratios are likely to decline in these industries and asset-to-market ratios and market equity are likely to rise. Then, ceteris paribus, he should include all three industries in his portfolio since their fundamentals point towards increased returns.

It might be appreciated by now that the discussion in this section could go on and on presenting and analysing different scenaria based on the models derived in this book. However, this could well be the theme of another book since the combinations that might be derived are numerous and hence optimisation techniques will be required in order to obtain the desired combinations.

9.2.2. Usefulness of the Findings for Corporate Financiers

The cost of capital or discount rate is a critical factor used by corporate financiers in several projects which have discounted cash - flow valuation as their backbone, such as capital budgeting and the valuation of privately and publicly owned companies. Despite the fact that there is no consensus among practitioners regarding the right model to use for estimating the cost of capital, traditionally, most applications have been employing the CAPM, mainly due to its simplicity.

The findings of this book (chapters 5, 6, 7 and 8), however, indicate that apart from the market, there appear to be other factors which are important in explaining the stock returns of the industries analysed and hence they should be included in the estimation of the industry's cost of capital. More specifically, the models proposed in this book are, firstly, the traditional CAPM (chapter 4) and, secondly, three cost of equity models that are extensions of CAPM (chapters 5, 6 and 7 for the US and chapter 8 for the global economy).

Like in the previous section, which focused on the usefulness of the findings of this book regarding the investor and the portfolio manager, we demonstrate the usefulness of the findings for the corporate financier through examples. Consider again the model identified in chapter 7 for the water transportation industry, which looks like:

$$\textit{Excess Returns} = 0.0334 + 0.9438 \times XR_M + 0.0037 \times ME - 0.0064 \times A/BE \;\; 0.5846 \times UMIP + 0.0406 \times UOG$$

Assume now that an investment banker is interested in valuing a private shipping company, which is interested to perform an initial public offering (IPO). The investment banker has to firstly calculate the cash flow stream that should be used to determine the value of the firm. This, in summary, is calculated as follows:

Free Cash Flow = (Earnings Before Interest and Tax) x (1-Tax rate)
+ Depreciation Expense
- Capital Expenditures
- Changes in Working Capital
+ Deferred Taxes

The free cash flow represents the funds that are flowing to the whole firm. Therefore, the appropriate discount rate to be used to calculate the value of the firm is the weighted average cost of capital (WACC). Free cash flow represents the stream of cash that the company generates that is translated into the company's ultimate value. It is the WACC that embodies the average expected return of all stake - holders in the company.

The weighted average cost of capital is calculated as follows:

$$WACC = Ke \times Ew + Kd \times (1 - t) \times Dw \qquad (9.3)$$

Where Ew is the weight of equity in the capital structure, Ke denotes the cost of equity, Dw is the weight of debt in the capital structure, Kd is the cost of debt, t denotes the marginal tax rate.

Table 9.3: Valuation of a Hypothetical Shipping Company

Assumptions:

Cash Flows $100 million per annum/annuity - like
Tax Rate 40%
Debt to Equity Ratio 1:1
Cost of Debt 8%

Cost of Equity:

Hypothetical Parameters used to calculate the cost of equity

XR_M	15%
UMIP	5%
UOG	20%
A/BE	0.7
ME	15

Cost of Equity:

a. Using the CAPM of chapter 4:
$Ke = 0.0336 + 0.9550 \times XR_M = 17.69\%$

b. Using the Multifactor Model of chapter 7:
$Ke = 0.0334 + 0.9438 \times XR_M - 0.5846 \times UMIP + 0.0406 \times OG - 0.0064 \times A/BE + 0.0037 \times ME$
$= 20.49\%$

Weighted Average Cost of Capital:

a. Using the CAPM cost of equity

$$WACC = Ke \times Ew + Kd \times (1 - t) \times Dw$$

$$= 17.69\% \times 1/2 + 8\% \times 60\% \times 1/2 = 11.2\%$$

b. Using the Multifactor Model cost of equity

$$WACC = Ke \times Ew + Kd \times (1 - t) \times Dw$$

$$= 20.49\% \times 1/2 + 8\% \times 60\% \times 1/2 = 12.6\%$$

Value of the Company:

a. Using the CAPM based WACC
Value = Cash Flows/WACC = 100/11.2% = $790

b. Using the Multifactor Model based WACC
Value = Cash Flows/WACC = 100/12.6% = $890

Difference in Value = $100 million*

* The difference in value is entirely due to the difference in the cost of equity.

One can therefore deduce how critical the inclusion of an accurate cost of equity is in estimating the WACC and how important, in turn, this is in estimating the value of the hypothetical private shipping company.

In the simplified example depicted in table 9.3, assume that our company is expected to generate annuity - like cash flows of $100 million per year, that its cost of debt is 8%, its tax rate is 40% and that its debt to equity ratio is 1:1. Using the simple one - factor model - CAPM (allowing the market factor to vary) described in chapter 4, a cost of equity of 17.69% is obtained, whereas, using the model described above (allowing the micro and macro economic factors to vary) a cost of equity of 20.49% is obtained. The former translates into a WACC of 11.2% while the latter into one of 12.6%. These, in turn, translate into value of $790 million (100/11.2%) and $890 (100/12.6%) million respectively. Needless to say that to most investment bankers, differences of this magnitude are material.

Similar examples may be cited using the other seven industries analysed in this book. Nevertheless, the above example has done more than enough to show that the multifactor models employed in this book could, indeed, be of use for the investment banker. Given its importance in investment banking decision making, practitioners require a cost of equity model that is generally accepted by other practitioners, easy to use in practical situations and accurate i.e. do not produce negative numbers or numbers exceeding 100%. It is our belief that the models employed in this book fulfil the above criteria.

9.3. Conclusion

Having summarised the major findings of the book we conclude this chapter with an overview of the findings. Firstly, as might be observed from table 9.1, chapters 4 to 7 conclude that the systematic risk, as measured by beta, of the US water transportation industry is not higher than unity, the beta of the "average" company. Moreover, chapters 5, 6 and 7 indicate that, if anything, the beta of this industry is lower than unity, the beta of the "average" company. The first part of chapter 4 does not share this finding, possibly due to the fact that the analysis was carried out during a marginally different time - period, utilising a different sample of companies and a different econometric methodology. Nevertheless, the findings of that part of the chapter do not indicate, in any way, that the beta of the shipping industry is higher than the beta of the market.

Secondly, with the exception of the first part of chapter 4, all other chapters indicate that the US water transportation industry, along with all other industries analysed, appears to have a significant positive alpha i.e. it is underpriced over the time horizon studied. The underpricing of the water transportation industry is in the range 3% - 4% depending on the model specification and, generally speaking, it is the industry exhibiting the highest underpricing among the transportation industries under review. Of the other industries analysed, electricity and gas appear to exhibit the highest underpricing.

Thirdly, chapters 5, 6 and 7 show that there are microeconomic and macroeconomic factors, in addition to the market, which have explanatory power over the returns of the industries analysed. Regarding microeconomic factors, chapter 5 suggests that there is a negative "asset-to-book value of equity" effect in the US water transportation industry while chapter 7 confirms this but also argues that there is a positive "size" effect in the industry. As far as macroeconomic factors are concerned, chapter 6 indicates a negative "industrial production" effect and a positive "oil prices" effect. These are confirmed in chapter 7.

Regarding the remaining industries, the sensitivities of each industry's returns to the set of microeconomic and macroeconomic factors employed varies. All factors, except the price to earnings ratio and inflation, appear to be priced in one industry or another. It should also be noted that, as might be observed from table 9.2.A. and 9.2.B, the sign of the microeconomic and macroeconomic factors utilised is mostly, but not always, in line with the majority of the existing literature.

The extension of the investigation to global industries in chapter 8 was made possible by the existence of global industry indices constructed by Morgan Stanley. The results are useful to global portfolio managers. It seems that the formation of global industry portfolios increases the exposures to market fluctuations for transportation and other industries in comparison to domestic US portfolios, as shown by the estimated values of market betas in chapter 8. Caution should be placed on this conclusion however, as the result may be dependent on the composition of the Morgan Stanley global indices, which have been used for the analysis. Also, as with domestic - US, industry portfolios indicate that global macroeconomic factors are significant in explaining industry returns, with the effect of each factor varying amongst global industries.

Finally, examples of the usefulness of the findings in this book for investment managers, who are interested in building diversified portfolios, and for corporate financiers, who are interested in the valuation of companies in individual industries, is demonstrated with practical examples.

In closing the book, it is worth mentioning here the results of some recent research by Kavussanos et al (2001) regarding the behaviour of shipping and shipping related company stock returns to reveal whether systematic risk differs across sectors of the shipping industry. Following an extensive collection of information through a postal questionnaire survey, 108 worldwide listed shipping and shipping related companies are classified by sector according to their core business activity. The CAPM is employed for the period 1996 to 1999 to model stock returns and compare sector β's. It is found that the systematic risks of the Drilling and Offshore sectors are significantly different from the systematic risks of all other sectors but not from each other. There seems to be no significant difference between the systematic risks of the Bulk, Tanker, Container and Ferry sectors. The systematic risk of the Cruise sector lies somewhere between these two groups. No significant difference could be found in the systematic risk of companies that diversified within shipping or shipping related industries when compared to companies which diversified in other areas.

Numerous variations and extensions, of the research presented in this book, could be made in the process of investigating the questions of industry equity returns, particularly for shipping, transportation and other industries. It is hoped that this book, by collecting a number of methodologies together, will provide the basis upon which to build further empirical work in the area, particularly in considering the issue of pricing of the factors unveiled in this book as possible determinants of industry returns.

References:

Air Industry Overview, (1995), Standard & Poor's Industry Surveys, http://www.library. upenn.edu/resources/databases/about/SandPIndSur.html

Akaike, H. (1973), 'Information theory and the extension of maximum likelihood principle', in Petrov, N. and Csaki, F. (eds), 'Proceedings of the second international symposium on information theory', Budapest, Akademiai Kiado, pp. 267-281.

Arditti, F. (1967), 'Risk and the Required Rate of Return', Journal of Finance, 22, pp.19-36.

Ball, R. (1978), 'Anomalies in relationships between securities', yields and yield – surrogates', Journal of Financial Economics, 6, pp. 103 - 126.

Banerjee, A., Dolado, J., Galbraith, J.W., and Hendry, D.F.(1993), 'Co-integration, error- correction, and the econometric analysis of non-stationary data', Oxford University Press, New York.

Banz, R. (1981), 'The relationship between returns and market value of common stocks', Journal of Financial Economics, 9, pp. 3 - 18.

Basu, S. (1977), 'Investment performance of common stocks in relation to the price - earnings ratios: A test of the efficient market hypothesis', Journal of Finance, 32, pp. 663 - 682.

Basu, S. (1983), 'The relationship between earnings, yield, market value and the return for NYSE common stocks: Further evidence', Journal of Financial Economics, 12, No 1.

Begg, D., Fisher, S., and Dornbusch, R. (1997), 'Economics', 5th edition, London: McGraw-Hill.

Bernard, V. (1986), 'Unanticipated Inflation and the Value of the Firm', Journal of Financial Economics, 15, pp. 285-321.

Berry, M., Burmeister, E., and McElroy, M. (1988), 'Sorting out Risks Using Known APT Factors', Financial Analysts Journal, March-April 1988, pp.29-43.

Bhandari, L. (1988), 'Debt - Equity ratio and expected common stock returns: Empirical evidence', Journal of Finance, 43, pp. 507 - 529.

Bong - Soo Lee (1992), 'Causal relations among stock returns, interest rates, real activity and inflation', Journal of Finance, 46, 4, pp. 1591 - 1603.

Boudoukh, J., Richardson, M., and Whitelaw, R. (1994), 'Industry returns and the Fisher effect', Journal of Finance, 49, 5, pp. 1595 - 1615.

Breeden, D. (1979), 'An intertemporal asset pricing model with stochastic consumption and investment opportunities', Journal of Financial Economics, 7, pp.256-296.

Brown, P., Kleidon, A., and Marsh, T. (1983), 'New evidence on the nature of size - related anomalies in stock prices', Journal of Financial Economics, 12, pp.33-56.

Burmeister, E., and Wall, K. (1986), 'The Arbitrage Pricing Theory and Macroeconomic Factor Measures', The Financial Review, Feb. 1986.

Burmeister, E., and McElroy, M. (1987), 'APT and multifactor asset pricing models with measures and unobserved factors: Theoretical and econometric issues', Discussion paper, Department of Economics, University of Virginia and Duke University.

Burmeister, E., and McElroy, M. (1988), 'Joint estimation of factor sensitivities and risk premia for the APT', Journal of Finance, 43, 3, pp. 721 - 733.

Campbell, J.Y., and Hamao, Y. (1989), 'Predictable Stock Returns in the United States and Japan:A Study of Long-Term Capital Market Integration', National Bureau of EconomicResearch Working Paper 3191, December 1989.

Capaul C. (1999), 'Asset Pricing Anomalies in Global Industry Indexes. Financial AnalystsJournal', July/August 1999, pp.17-37.

Capaul, C., Rowley, I., and Sharpe, W.F. (1993), 'International Value and Growth Stock Returns', Financial Analysts Journal, January/February 1993, pp.27-36.

Carleton, W., and Lakonishok, J. (1986), 'The Size Anomaly: Does Industry Group matter?', The Journal of Portfolio Management, Spring 1986, pp.36-40.

Chan, K., Chen N. and Hsieh D. (1985), 'An Exploratory Investigation of the Firm Size Effect', Journal of Financial Economics, 14, pp.451-471.

Chan, L., Hamao, Y., and Lakonishok, J. (1991), 'Fundamentals and stock returns in Japan', Journal of Finance, 46, pp. 1739 - 1789.

Chen, N. (1983), 'Some Empirical Tests of the Theory of Arbitrage Pricing', Journal of Finance, 38, pp.1393-1414.

Chen, N., Roll, R., and Ross, S. (1986), 'Economic forces and the stock market', Journal of Business, 59, pp.383 - 403.

Chen, J., and Jordan, D. (1993), 'Some empirical tests in the APT: Macrovariables versus derived factors', Journal of Banking and Finance, 17, pp. 65 - 89.

Damodaran, A. (1994), 'Damodaran on Valuation - Security Analysis for Investment and Corporate Finance', John Wiley & Sons Inc.

Dickey, D., and Fuller, W. (1979): 'Distribution of the Estimators for Autoregressive Time Series with a Unit Root', Journal of the American Statistical Association, 74, pp. 427 - 431.

Dickey, D., and Fuller, W. (1981): 'Likelihood Ratio Statistics for Autoregressive Time Series with a Unit Root', Econometrica, 49, pp.1057 - 1072.

Dumas, B., and Solnik, B. (1995), 'The World Price of Foreign Exchange Rate Risk', Journal of Finance, 2, pp.445-479.

Engerman, M. (1993), 'Using Fundamental and Economic Factors to Explain Stock Returns', BARRA Newsletter, Fall 1993.

Engle, F., and Granger, C. (1987), 'Cointegration and Error Correction: Representation, Estimation and Testing', Econometrica , 55, pp. 251-276.

Eun, C., and Resnick, B. (1992), 'Forecasting the correlation structure of share prices: A test of new models', Journal of Banking and Finance, 16, pp.643 - 656.

Fabozzi, F., and Francis, C. (1977), 'Stability Tests for Alphas and Betas over Bull and Bear Market Conditions', Journal of Finance, September 1977.

Fabozzi, F., and Francis, J. (1979), 'Industry Effects and the Determinants of Beta', The Quarterly Review of Economics and Business, 19, 3, pp.61-74.

Fama, E. (1970), 'Efficient Capital Markets: A Review of Theory and Empirical Work', Journal of Finance, 2, pp. 383-417.

Fama, E. (1976), 'Reply to Jensen, M. and Bennington, G', Journal of Finance, 1, pp. 143 - 145.

Fama, E. (1991), 'Efficient Capital Markets: II', Journal of Finance, 46, pp. 1575-1617.

Fama, E., and French, K. (1992), 'The cross - section of expected stock returns', Journal of Finance, 47, pp. 427 - 465.

Fama, E., and MacBeth, J. (1973), 'Risk return and equilibrium: Empirical tests' Journal of Political Economy, 81, pp. 607-636.

Ferson, W., and Harvey, C. (1991), 'The variation of economic risk premiums', Journal of Political Economy, 99, pp. 385 - 415.

Ferson, W., and Harvey, C. (1993), 'The Risk and Predictability of International Equity Returns',Review of Financial Studies, 6, pp.527-566.

Ferson, W., and Harvey, C. (1994), 'Sources of Risk and Expected Returns in Global Equity Markets', Journal of Banking and Finance, 18, pp.775-803.

Gallant, A. R. (1975), 'Seemingly unrelated nonlinear regressions', Journal of Econometrics, 3, pp. 35-50.

Gibbons, M. (1982), 'Multivariate tests of financial models: A new approach', Journal of Financial Economics, 10, pp. 3-27.

Gultekin, M.N. (1983), 'Stock Market Returns and Inflation: Evidence from other Countries', Journal of Finance, 38, pp.49-65.

Gultekin, M., Gultekin, N., and Penati A. (1989), 'Capital Controls and International Capital Market Segmentation: The Evidence from the Japanese and American Stock Markets', Journal of Finance, 44 pp.849-870.

Gyourko, J. and Keim, D. (1993), 'Risk and Return in Real Estate: Evidence from a Real Estate Index', Financial Analysts Journal, Sep.- Oct.1993, pp.39-46.

Hamao, Y. (1988), 'An empirical examination of the arbitrage pricing theory', Japan and the World Economy, 1, pp.45 - 61.

Hardouvelis, G. (1988), 'Stock prices: nominal versus real shocks', Financial Markets and Portfolio Management, 2, pp.10-18.

Harris, R. (1995), 'Using Cointegration Analysis in Econometric Modelling', Prentice Hall/Harvester Wheatsheaf

Harvey, C. (1991), 'The world price of covariance risk', Journal of Finance, 46, pp.111-157.

Isimbabi, M. (1994), 'The stock market perception of industry risk and the separation of banking and commerce', Journal of Banking and Finance, 18, pp. 325 - 349.

Jacobs, J. (1986), 'World Tanker Fleet Review', John, I. Jacobs & Co, London.

Jaffe, J., Keim, D., and Westerfield, R. (1989), 'Earnings yields, market values and stock returns', Journal of Finance, 44, pp.135-148.

Jones, C. (1993), 'Investments: Analysis and Management', 4th Edition, John Wiley & Sons Inc.

Judge, G. G., Hill, R. C., Griffiths, W. E., Lutkepohl, H., and Lee, T. C. (1988), 'Introduction to the theory and practice of econometrics', second edition, J. Wiley & Sons.

Kane, E., and Unal, H. (1988), 'Change in Market Assessment of Deposit-Institution Riskiness', Journal of Financial Services Research, 1, pp.207-229.

Kavussanos, M.G., and Marcoulis, S.N. (1995), 'Beta Comparisons Across Industries - A Water Transportation Industry perspective', Discussion paper No.16, International Centre for Shipping, Trade and Finance, City University Business School, London, UK.

Kavussanos, M.G., and Marcoulis, S. (1997a), 'Risk and Return of U.S. water transportation stocks over time and over bull and bear market conditions', Maritime Policy and Management, 24, 2, pp.145 - 158.

Kavussanos, M., and Marcoulis, S. (1997b), 'The stock market perception of industry risk and microeconomic factors: The case of the US water transportation industry versus other industries', Transportation Research, Part E, 33, 2, pp.147 - 158.

Kavussanos, M.G., and Marcoulis, S. (1997c), 'Risk, Return and Investment Decisions', Lloyd's Shipping Economist, Capital for Shipping, 1997, pp.8 - 11.

Kavussanos, M.G., and Marcoulis, S. (1998), 'Beta comparisons across industries - A water transportation industry perspective', Maritime Policy and Management, 25, 2, pp.175 - 184.
Also, presented at the UK Chamber of Shipping, 18 May 1998.

Kavussanos, M.G., and Marcoulis, S. (2000a), 'The stock market perception of industry and macroeconomic factors: The case of the US water transportation industry versus other transport industries', International Journal of Maritime Economics, 2, 3, pp.235 – 256.
Also, presented at the International Association of Maritime Economists (IAME) Conference, Vancouver, Canada, 26-28 June 1996.

Kavussanos, M.G., and Marcoulis, S. (2000b), 'The stock market perception of industry risk through the use of a multifactor model', International Journal of Transport Economics, XXVII, 1, pp.77 – 98.
Also, presented at the International Association of Maritime Economists (IAME) Conference, London, UK, 22-24 September 1997.

Kavussanos, M.G., Juell-Skielse, A. and Forrest, M., 'International comparison of market risks across subsectors of the shipping industry', IAME2001 conference, Hong Kong.

Keim, D. (1983), 'Size Related Anomalies and Stock Market Seasonality: Further Empirical Evidence' Journal of Financial Economics, pp.13-32.

King, B. (1966), 'Market and industry factors in stock price behaviour', Journal of Business, 39, pp.139 - 190.

Lakonishok, J., and Shapiro, A. (1986), 'Systematic risk, total risk and size as determinants of stock market returns', Journal of Business Finance, 10, 1, pp.115 - 132.

Levy, R. (1974), 'Beta Coefficients as Predictors of Returns', Financial Analysts Journal, Jan-Feb, pp. 61-69.

Lintner, J. (1965), 'The valuation of risk assets and the selection of risky investments in stock portfolios and capital budgets', Review of Economics and Statistics, 47, pp. 13-37.

Lintner, J. (1965), 'Security Prices, Risk, and Maximal Gains from Diversification', Journal of Finance, Dec, pp.587 - 615.

Lucas, R. (1978), 'Asset prices in an exchange economy', Econometrica, 46, pp.1429-1445.

MacKinnon, J.G. (1991), 'Critical values for cointegration tests', in Engle, R.F. and C.W.J. Granger (eds.), 'Long-run economic relationships', Oxford University Press, Oxford.

Magnus, J. R. (1978), 'Maximum likelihood estimation of the GLS model with unknown parameters in the disturbance covariance matrix', Journal of Econometrics, 7, pp. 281-312.

Martinez, A., and Rubio, J. (1989), 'Arbitrage pricing with macroeconomic variables: An empirical investigation using Spanish data', Working Chapter, Universidad del Pais Vasco.

National Energy Policy Plan, (1995), Chapter 4: 'Sustainable Energy Strategy - clean and secure energy for a competitive economy', July 1995, National Energy Policy Plan, Pursuant to Section 801 of the Department of Energy Organization Act, US. http://www.nttc.edu/env/titlepg.html.

Nerlove, M. (1968), 'Factors Affecting Differences Among Rates of Return on Investment in Individual Common Stocks', Review of Economics and Statistics, 50, pp.312-331.

Neuberger, J. (1991), 'Risk and Return in Banking: Evidence from Bank Stock Returns', Federal Reserve Bank of San Francisco Economic Review, pp.18-39.

Pearce, D., and Roley, V. (1985), 'Stock prices and economic news,' Journal of Business, 58, 1, pp. 49 - 67.

Pindyck, R., and Rubinfeld, D. (1991): 'Econometric Models and Economic Forecasts,' 3rd edition, McGraw-Hill International Editions, Singapore.

Poon, S., and Taylor, S.J. (1991), 'Macroeconomic factors and the UK stock market', Journal of Business, Finance and Accounting, 18, pp. 619 - 636.

Porter, M. (1980), 'Competitive Strategy: Techniques for Analysing Industries and Competitors', 1980, Free Press.

Rail Industry Overview, (1995), Standard & Poor's Industry Surveys, http://www. library.upenn.edu/resources/databases/about/SandPIndSur.html

Reinganum, M. (1981), 'Mis - specification of capital asset pricing: Empirical anomalies based on earnings yields and market values', Journal of Financial Economics, 9, pp.19 - 46.

Reinganum, M. (1982), 'A direct test of Roll's conjecture on the firm size effect', Journal of Finance, 37, pp.27-36.

Reinganum, M. (1986), 'Misspecification of Capital Asset Pricing', Journal of Finance, September, 41, 4, pp.779-793.

Resources for the Future, (1997), 'A Shock to the System: Restructuring America's Electricity Industry', Washington, DC. http://www.rff.org/resources_articles/files/ electdereg.htm

Roll, R. (1977), 'A critique of the asset pricing theory's tests, Part I: On past and potential testability of the theory', Journal of Financial Economics, 4, pp.129 - 176.

Roll, R. (1981), 'A possible explanation of the small firm effect', Journal of Finance, 36, pp.879-888.

Roll, R. (1992), 'Industrial Structure and the Comparative Behaviour of International Stock Market Indices', Journal of Finance, 47 pp.3-42.

Roll, R., and Ross S. (1980), 'An Empirical Investigation of the Arbitrage Pricing Theory', Journal of Finance, 35 pp.1073-1103.

Rosenberg, B., Kenneth, R., and Lanstein, R. (1985), 'Persuasive evidence of market inefficiency', Journal of Portfolio Management, 11, pp. 9 - 17.

Rosenberg, J. (1991), 'The New Japanese Equity Model', BARRA Newsletter, November/December.

Ross, S. (1976), 'The arbitrage theory of capital asset pricing', Journal of Economic Theory, 13, pp. 341-360.

Rouwenhorst, K.G. (1999), 'European Equity Markets and the EMU', Financial Analysts Journal, May/June, pp. 57-64.

Roy, V. (1992), 'BARRA Releases New Canadian Model', BARRA Newsletter, March/April.

Rubinstein, M. (1976), 'The valuation of uncertain income streams and the pricing of options', Bell Journal of Economics and Management Science, 7, pp.407-425.

Saunders, A., and Yourougou, P. (1990), 'Are banks special? The separation of banking and commerce', Journal of Economics and Business, 42, pp.171 - 182.

Schwarz, G. (1978), 'Estimating the Dimension of a Model,' Annals of Statistics, 6, pp. 461 - 464.

Sharpe, W. (1964), 'Capital Asset Prices: A theory of market equilibrium under conditions of risk' Journal of Finance, pp. 425 - 442.

Sharpe, W., Alexander, G., and Bailey, J. (1995), 'Investments', 5th Edition, Prentice Hall International Editions.

Simanoff, D., (1998), 'Can Real Estate soar while Wall Street bears roar? Tampa Bay Business Journal, October.

Smith, A. [1776] (1986), 'The Wealth of Nations', Penguin Classics, Penguin Books Ltd, London.

Sorensen, E., and Burke, T. (1986), 'Portfolio returns from active industry group rotation', Financial Analysts Journal, September - October 1986.

Stambaugh, R. (1982), 'On the exclusion of assets from tests of the two-parameter model', Journal of Financial Economics, 10, pp. 237-268.

Stattman, D. (1980), 'Book value and stock returns', The Chicago MBA: A Journal of Selected Chapters, University of Chicago, 4, pp.25 - 45.

Stoll, H., and Whaley, R. (1983), 'Transaction costs and the small firm effect', Journal of Financial Economics, 12, pp.57-80.

Stopford, M. (1997), 'Maritime Economics', Routledge, London.

The Jones Act Reform Coalition Report, (1998), http://www.mctf.com/jonesact.htm

Transportation Industry Study Report (1996), 'Technology and Industrial Base Sector Studies', ICAF (Industrial College of the Armed Forces) Publications, National DefenseUniversity,Washington,DC.http://www.dtic.mil/natibo/docs/TechIndBaseFull.html# trans96.

Theil, H. (1971), 'Principles of Econometrics', New York, Wiley.

Thierer, A. D. (1997), 'A Free Market in Electricity: Will Michigan Get It Right?', Mackinac Center for Public Policy, US.

Wasserfallen, W. (1989), 'Macroeconomic news and the stock market - Evidence from Europe', Journal of Banking and Finance, 13, pp.613 - 626.

Weiss, R.A. (1998), 'Global Sector Rotation: New Look at an Old Idea', Financial Analysts Journal, May/June, pp.6-8.

Zellner, A. (1962), 'An efficient method of estimating Seemingly Unrelated Regressions and tests of aggregation bias', Journal of the American Statistical Association, 57, pp.348-368.

Ziobrowski, B., and Ziobrowski, A. (1995), 'Exchange Rate Risk and Internationally Diversified Portfolios', Journal of International Money and Finance, 14, pp.65-81.

INDEX OF AUTHORS

INDEX OF SUBJECTS

GPSR Compliance
The European Union's (EU) General Product Safety Regulation (GPSR) is a set of rules that requires consumer products to be safe and our obligations to ensure this.

If you have any concerns about our products, you can contact us on

ProductSafety@springernature.com

In case Publisher is established outside the EU, the EU authorized representative is:

Springer Nature Customer Service Center GmbH
Europaplatz 3
69115 Heidelberg, Germany

www.ingramcontent.com/pod-product-compliance
Ingram Content Group UK Ltd.
Pitfield, Milton Keynes, MK11 3LW, UK
UKHW021607110926
15112UKWH00017B/119

* 9 7 8 1 4 7 5 7 6 4 4 2 0 *